This book is an easy-to-read, practical guide on managing sexual harassment issues in the workplace. Drawing from the author's 30 years of experience in the field of employment discrimination law, the book provides step-by-step instructions on how to avoid and resolve sexual harassment situations before somebody files a lawsuit.

—**U.S. Rep. Robert C. Scott** (D-VA)

Linda Howard has produced a wonderfully practical book to help guide employers and their employees in thinking about sexual harassment in the workplace. Down to earth and not judgmental, the book provides an effective way to approach these issues that is likely to lead to understanding of how to avoid problems, recognize them if you have them, and to resolve them before calling a lawyer. I will certainly use it.

—**Steve Koblik**, president, The Huntington Library

Sexual harassment continues to be a complex issue in today's workplaces. Linda Gordon Howard's book is an important and necessary resource to help us understand sexual harassment from legal, management, and social science perspectives.

Her focus is on understanding when sexual harassment is occurring and what to do immediately following an incident. Howard brings her 30 years of expertise as an attorney, trainer, and teacher to helping us understand what sexual harassment is and isn't and what managers must do to keep employees safe. She has a wonderful ability to explain profound ideas in a way that is accessible as well as helpful to individuals. Howard's book is absolutely essential reading for all of us.

—**Dr. Michele Paludi**, editor of *Ivory Power:
Sexual Harassment on College Campuses*
and co-editor of *Academic and Workplace Sexual
Harassment*

Linda Gordon Howard devotes an exceptional range of experience and expertise to tackling the menace of sexual harassment in the workplace. This book is a practical guide for supervisors and employees, and explains the black, white and gray of sexual harassment, negative workplace culture, and how to create a safe work environment. No office should be without this book.

  —Sheila Jackson Lee, member of Congress, Texas,
    18th Congressional District

*I wish I had Linda Gordon Howard's book before they gave me a perp walk when I first heard of sexual harassment. **The Sexual Harassment Handbook** clears up the mystery. This book is a practical guide to avoiding problems and resolving difficult sexual situations at work. It's readable and full of fascinating stories about the crazy things people do instead of just talking to each other, paying attention and respecting other people's boundaries. It promises to be a book anyone can use, and it delivers brilliantly.*

  —Peter Norton, philanthropist and creator of
    Norton Utilities and Norton Antivirus computer
    software

THE

SEXUAL HARASSMENT HANDBOOK

Protect Yourself and Coworkers From the
Realities of Sexual Harassment

Take Action, Investigate, and Remedy
Accusations of Harassment

Create Corporate Policies That Educate
and Empower Employees

LINDA GORDON HOWARD

Attorney At Law

CAREER
PRESS
Franklin Lakes, NJ

THE SEXUAL HARASSMENT HANDBOOK
EDITED BY DIANNA WALSH
TYPESET BY EILEEN DOW MUNSON
Cover design by Johnson Design
Printed in the U.S.A. by Book-mart Press

To order this title, please call toll-free 1-800-CAREER-1 (NJ and Canada: 201-848-0310) to order using VISA or MasterCard, or for further information on books from Career Press.

CAREER
PRESS

The Career Press, Inc., 3 Tice Road, PO Box 687,
Franklin Lakes, NJ 07417
www.careerpress.com

Library of Congress Cataloging-in-Publication Data

Available upon request.

Acknowledgments

This book is a creation of and a testament to the power of one person's dream. My dream stayed alive because there were many, many people who listened to me, supported me, and believed in my dream to write a book about sexual harassment that people could really use to make life at work better. I thank and acknowledge each and every person who listened and allowed my dream to be real for them.

I thank my mother, Dr. Vivian G. Howard, my best friend, chief cheerleader, and most persistent nudge. Mom proofread the book proposal, critiqued the first draft of the manuscript and stayed up with me later than she should have while I made the final edits.

I thank my wonderful literary agent, Lisa Hagan, whom I had the good fortune to meet on an Amtrak train from New York to Petersburg, Virginia. Since the moment Lisa entered my life, she has been welcoming, encouraging, and unwavering in her belief in me and this book.

I thank my author friends, David Allyn, Sally Batson, and Elizabeth Foster, who gave generously of their time to read the early drafts and help me craft my message.

I acknowledge the staff and program leaders of Landmark Education, especially my fellow seminar leaders, for being my partners in transforming what is possible for human beings. They are my partners in creating a world where no one suffers and where everyone grows and thrives. They encouraged me to find my own voice and to speak to the world.

I acknowledge my good friends and the volunteers at A More Perfect Union, Inc., especially Jamie Allen Black and Sarala Dee, who told me endlessly that my dreams can come true. I am especially grateful to Jamie for typing the first draft of this book.

I am grateful to everyone who offered ideas and shared what they wanted in a book about sexual harassment. Peter Norton was good enough to remind to bring some humor to the topic. Dan Greenberg asked me to make the book short enough to read. Dean Barbara Fife asked for a chapter that would tell her exactly what to do if someone came to her with a complaint. Martha Mann Alfaro asked the hard questions. Virtually every person who sat next to me on a train or airplane over the last several years contributed their experiences of sexual harassment at work and in school.

Contents

Introduction

Our national fascination with sexual harassment began the October weekend in 1991 when the U.S. Senate Judiciary Committee conducted hearings to investigate Oklahoma University Law School Professor Anita Hill's allegations of sexual harassment by her former employer and then Supreme Court nominee Clarence Thomas. Virtually everyone watched, and nearly everyone had an opinion about whether Professor Hill was telling the truth and whether Clarence Thomas should have been denied a seat on the Supreme Court, even if he had made sexual comments to Professor Hill while he was her supervisor. Yet few people, other than experts in sexual harassment law, could define what sexual harassment was. During that long weekend of televised hearings, neither the Senate Judiciary Committee, nor the news organizations covering it, made an effort to educate the senators or the public about the nature and definition of sexual harassment.

Sexual harassment emerged as national news again in 1997, and continuing into 1998, when Paula Jones's sexual harassment lawsuit against President Bill Clinton exposed allegations that President Clinton engaged in sexual activity with Monica Lewinsky, an intern at the White House, and led to

President Clinton's admission that he had an "inappropriate" relationship with her. This time the focus was on whether the President lied in his grand jury testimony and in his broadcast statements to the nation when he denied having sexual relations with Ms. Lewinsky.

One after another, stories emerge about powerful and ordinary people being accused of sexual harassment with tragic consequences for the victim, themselves, and their families. Most working people, no matter how successful, intelligent, or well intentioned, do not understand the law of sexual harassment. Some people resent the interference with their personal relationships and refuse to constrain themselves in any way. Others abandon judgment in the face of sexually charged situations. Some men choose to protect themselves by avoiding any kind of personal comments toward the opposite sex. Many women suffer sexually harassing situations in silence, unaware of their rights and unprepared to deal with the situation.

The Anita Hill–Clarence Thomas story and, later, the Monica Lewinsky–Bill Clinton story, so fascinated the public because they showed "sex talk" and scandal played out at the highest levels of government. Sex, misbehavior, and celebrity fascinate us. A story that includes all three captures our attention.

Despite a vast system of laws prohibiting sexual harassment and growing awareness about sexual harassment, the currently available tools do not acknowledge the biological and social fact that when people work together, sexual attraction and sexual behavior are inevitable. The major tool available to address unwanted sexual attention at work is an adversarial system. One employee accuses another employee.

The accused employee defends himself. The accused employee is vindicated or fired. The accusing employee may sue the employer. The lawsuit takes years to resolve, during which time the accusing employee may quit his or her job. The employer may pay money. There are few resources or methods to help workers to deal effectively in the difficult moments when sex and power converge.

I have spent thousands of hours talking with people in sexual harassment training workshops, counseling sessions, meetings, and legal briefings. One thing that became very clear was that situations involving sexual harassment almost always come as a surprise. All the activity happened after the fact. It is as if someone was walking down the street, doing what he or she does everyday, then suddenly wakes up in a nightmare of upset, confusion, resentment, and fear. The job is to pick up the pieces.

Working people need guidance in how to deal with sex-related situations they face everyday: the man who wants to approach a woman but wants to avoid sexually harassing her; the woman who wants to tell someone to leave her alone but doesn't know how; the coworker who sees another employee being treated badly but doesn't know what to say; the manager who receives a complaint but doesn't know how to respond; the man who is accused of sexual harassment and fears losing his job; and the employer who wants to avoid sex-related lawsuits. This book describes what and whom to look for, how to communicate effectively, and what to do when traditional communication does not work.

People who work have to contend with vague and ineffective communication, outmoded sexual and courtship rituals, sexual stereotypes and gender-based work roles, abuses of power by supervisors, group intimidation, lack of deterrents, and organizational indifference.

I designed this book to be an easy-to-read reference tool that gives you step-by-step instructions for interactions on the job that involve human sexuality, miscommunication, and misuse of power.

This book offers the possibility of safe working environments, where men and women work together cooperatively and professionally, and can even pursue personal relationships without the dark cloud of sexual harassment hanging over every conversation and gesture. In some instances, someone will call a lawyer and the adversarial system will kick in. But there are vast opportunities to alter the course of events before that happens. If you follow the guidelines in this book, you will have an advantage before someone calls a lawyer.

Studies show that:

- A typical Fortune 500 Company loses $6.7 million per year in absenteeism, low productivity, and employee turnover because of sexual harassment.

- The average jury award in a sexual harassment lawsuit is $450,000.

- One of every two sexual harassers is the victim's supervisor.

- Nearly one out of every two people who experience sexual harassment does and says nothing about it because of the fear of being punished, disbelieved, or ignored.

- Ninety-five out of every 100 working women have received sexual material, such as letters and phone calls, at work.
- Nine out of every 10 sexually harassed women suffer from debilitating stress reactions, including depression, headaches, and other physical symptoms.

The gender gap

Men and women had differing opinions about Anita Hill's story and had very different views of the effect it should have on Judge Clarence Thomas's nomination to be a Justice of the Supreme Court. (Of course, the Senate did confirm Thomas, and he joined the Court a few weeks later.)

Men, by and large, thought Hill was lying, or thought that, even if she were telling the truth, an incident that might or might not have happened 10 years ago should not affect Thomas's pending appointment to the Supreme Court. Women, with few exceptions, believed that Hill was telling the truth and that Thomas did not belong on the nation's highest court.

That single episode exposed the vast gender gap between how most men and most women view sexual harassment. The difference in men's and women's views on sexual harassment has also been reported in studies. *The New York Times* published the results of a nationwide study of employees in 12 companies who were asked questions about their experiences of sexual harassment in the preceding year. Of those responding, 43 percent of women and 9 percent of men said they had experienced "sexual teasing" at work. A full 98 percent of women and only one percent of men said they had received letters, phone calls, cartoons, or other materials of a sexual nature.

The difference in perception of sexual harassment between men and women does not represent an inherent failure of men, but rather a difference in experience and exposure.

Typically, men run companies and make decisions about personnel policy, and, as a result, many women are skeptical about their employer's ability and willingness to enforce policies prohibiting sexual conduct in the workplace. There are a number of reasons why men, in particular, often don't recognize sexual harassment when it occurs and sometimes do not consider it to be a serious workplace issue. Sexual harassment typically occurs in private or as a series of incidents over time, and the vast majority of men have neither observed it nor experienced it personally. Women often experience behavior as intimidating, offensive, or hostile that men do not experience in the same way. While men can be harassed, the vast majority of sexual harassment is visited upon women by a minority of men. Much sexual harassment is not reported, and women often leave their jobs or endure the harassment without ever mentioning the problem.

These factors tend to make sexual harassment invisible to two critical groups: the people who cause it and the people who are responsible for doing something about it. In the vast majority of organizations, men dominate both groups. As more women have expressed their concerns about unwanted behavior, men have gained a greater appreciation for their experience and the magnitude of the issue.

Sexual harassment has become an issue because of recent changes in the law, and we have to turn to the law to define harassment. In reality, sexual harassment is a human phenomenon that happens between human beings. Sexual harassment is defined and clarified in court cases, but sexual harassment doesn't happen in court. By the time people realize that they are dealing with sexual harassment, it is often too late. The lawyers have arrived, the positions have been staked out, and the battle has begun.

We are all in the same boat

Think of your workplace as a ship sailing across the Atlantic Ocean. Your mission is to measure the air currents at sea. Everyone on board takes a turn at the wheel, as well as another job related to the task. You can take any route you want, you just have to keep sailing and measuring the air currents. If you sail too close to the North Pole, the weather will get too cold for some of the people. Their fingers won't be able to operate the equipment, and they will eventually get too sick or discouraged to work. If they get too cold, they will stay below deck or leave on a life raft and head south for relief.

Some people steer to the north when it's their turn at the wheel. They have nice warm coats and find cold sea air refreshing. A few can't read a compass and sail north by accident. Others enjoy watching the warm-blooded people squirm. Whatever their reasons, little by little, the ship heads north. The warm-blooded people start to huddle below deck and sneak away in the lifeboats. Some haven't been seen for days and are believed to have jumped overboard in desperation.

No matter where the ship goes, everyone is in the same boat. Unless everyone works together, speaking up when they are cold, asking how cold is too cold, demanding that everyone head in the direction of a temperate zone, removing people who are endangering the mission from the controls, and training people how to read a compass, and sending those who don't cooperate to the lifeboats, the mission fails.

There is little value to the mission in finding out how far north you can go without hitting an iceberg. In the same way, there is little value to any organization in finding out how much sexual behavior can you engage in before you cross the line into sexual harassment. A little brisk air is refreshing from time to time, as is a little flirtation, but the northern route is treacherous, costly, and harmful to some of the crew. You have to establish a route that works for you and the people with whom you work. You have to make periodic, regular, and timely course corrections. Everyone has a role.

This book is for real people who have real jobs and have to deal with real situations everyday. It is not about how to win a lawsuit or how to prepare for a lawsuit. It gives practical advice for what to do before you confront a situation involving sexual harassment.

Rather than criticizing men, I urge women and men to share more openly their experiences with and concerns about maintaining personal boundaries in the workplace. Rather than eliminating all sexual banter and playfulness, which I think gives us sterile humorless workplaces, I urge communicating to discover one another's personal boundaries and how our actions affect our fellow workers. It is possible to work together as human beings who value each other, even flirt and joke together, while steering clear of offensive behavior.

Creating workplaces with healthy communication between men and women and honor for the dignity of every employee calls for transforming fundamental aspects of how men and women relate to one another at work. If you follow the simple guidelines in this book, you will learn how to read the compass and how to chart your course.

What to expect in this book

In Part I, I will define sexual harassment in simple practical terms and illustrate how the definition applies in common workplace situations. I will describe in detail some of the sexual harassment cases that have resulted in big verdicts and settlements against employers, as well as some of the cases in which employers prevailed.

In Part II, I will list and explore effective actions you can take when you think you've been harassed, when you want to avoid harassing a colleague, and when you have been accused of harassing someone. Also, you will find step-by-step guidance for responding to a subordinate or coworker who complains to you about sexual harassment, what to expect when you have been asked to cooperate in an investigation, and other common workplace situations where sexual harassment could be involved.

Part III proposes a strategy for preventing sexual harassment in the workplace that can be customized to any workplace, and in which there is a role for any worker who has interest in taking part. You will find guidance for the special problems of sexual misbehavior in unique environments, including educational institutions, the military, and the church. The primary focus here is on issues facing working people.

Domestic abuse, incest, and sexual molestation of children, while critically important problems, will not be addressed to any significant degree.

Finally, in Chapter 15 I will propose changes in how we communicate and deal with power and sexuality at work. We can begin to break free from outdated ways of interacting that no longer work. With better relationships at work, we can begin to unleash and redirect untapped energies of the American worker and cause an unprecedented surge in work-place productivity and satisfaction.

Part I

• • •

The Reality
of
Sexual
Harassment

1

Power, Sex, and Romance on the Job

During a workshop on sexual harassment prevention I was leading for employees of a Fortune 500 corporation, one of the participants, an engineer, spoke up. He said, "I spend more time at work than I spend anywhere else. In a 24-hour day, I spend eight hours sleeping, half an hour dressing, two hours traveling, an hour eating dinner, and nine or 10 hours here at work. Not counting weekends, I have only about two hours a day to meet women and socialize. I'm a single guy. Where am I supposed to meet women to go out with, if I can't meet them at work?"

He had a point. Dating at work is not a new phenomenon. Romantic liaisons, both happy and unhappy, are common in the workplace. We all have seen examples of successful romantic relationships that developed at work. Managers marry other employees; college professors marry colleagues.

When men and women work together, sexual interest and sexual advances are inevitable. Romance and sex on the job work for some people.

On the other hand, abusive relationships and exploitive situations also exist at work. Somewhere between are situations that are neither happy nor seriously injurious. Sexual harassment comes in a wide variety of behaviors. Women find unwelcome pornographic pictures and cartoons on their desks. Studies show that 95 in 100 women workers receive sexual material at work, such as letters, pictures, telephone calls, and e-mails. Two thirds of the people responding to one study said they had been sexually harassed on the job. Other studies also show that nearly half of the employees who believe they've experienced sexual harassment say or do nothing about it.

Laws that prohibit sexual harassment in the workplace require workers to separate different kinds of sexual interactions. It seems like a simple thing to do, but often, it is not simple at all.

Several years ago, I met a woman I'll call "Joan" at a friend's baby shower. Joan told me the following story:

"I used to work as a secretary in a small real estate office in New Jersey. Just the two of us worked there, the real estate agent, who was my boss, and me. I had worked for him for about a year when one day, out of the blue, he asked me to come into the conference room and watch a movie with him. It was a strange request. There was never any reason for me to go into the conference room. He had meetings in there. I asked him what kind of movie it was. I thought it might be a real estate movie or a training film.

"He said, 'Well, you know. I think you'll enjoy it.'

"I still didn't know what he was talking about, so I asked him again, what the movie was.

"He said, 'Come on, Joan. We'll have a little fun. This will loosen you up a little.'

"Suddenly, I knew he was talking about a pornographic movie. I couldn't believe it. I was so shocked and embarrassed that I left and never came back to work. To this day, I wonder what I did to make him think that I would do anything like that. I was single then. I'm married now, and I never told my husband about this guy. I never told anyone before now."

•   •   •

Joan's experience is typical. The person who approached her was her direct supervisor. Nearly one in every two harassers is the direct supervisor of the person he or she harasses. Joan asked for information about the specific nature of the movie, but her boss did not give her a straight answer. We'll never know whether it was a pornographic movie. The vague invitation would allow her boss to say, truthfully, that he never invited her to view a porn movie. Had Joan insisted on knowing what kind of movie it was, she risked accusing her boss of making an improper advance. The experience had a big impact on her. She left her job without saying anything to her boss about her embarrassment and upset.

Joan never reported the incident to any agency or professional group. Nearly half of victims of sexual harassment say or do nothing. Joan continues to wonder what she could have done to cause her boss to think that she might have been interested in watching an X-rated movie with him. People who experience sexual harassment sometimes leave their jobs out of embarrassment or fear. Many of them are left with a nagging guilt that they did something to encourage the behavior.

The point is that Joan's boss was serving his personal agenda ("to loosen her up") and would not be clear about what he wanted, leaving Joan intimidated and upset.

Joan's experience took place in a small office in New Jersey, but women in large corporations have similar experiences on a daily basis. For example, women in a major U.S. corporation complained in a 1995 lawsuit that they were regularly required to wear skimpy clothing to office parties, where they were expected to entertain clients and watch pornographic movies. Secretaries in the law firm of Baker and McKenzie endured the touches and pinches of a senior partner for years, while the management of the firm allowed the behavior to go on unchecked. Ultimately, both firms paid millions of dollars in legal fees and settlement costs after employees brought lawsuits.

What makes sexual harassment different from romance or harmless social conversation? The main difference is that romantic behavior is agreeable and pleasing to both people. There is usually a desire to please one another. Generally, both people respect and accept one another's wishes. In work situations, however, one party is often not free to object to another's behavior. In the relationship between a supervisor and a subordinate, the subordinate must follow the instructions of the supervisor or risk negative consequences, such as losing the job. We expect the supervisor to make demands that are related to business.

Problems arise when the supervisor has a personal agenda, unrelated to his or her business responsibilities. The supervisor who makes demands that serve a personal agenda and is not interested in the subordinate's wishes risks abusing the subordinate. Joan found herself in this type of situation. Another type of problem arises when one employee, not necessarily a supervisor, makes comments or engages in other behavior toward another employee that is offensive or disruptive.

A third type of problem arises when a social relationship between two employees ends and one of them attempts to resume the relationship over the other's objection. Groups of workers who resent a particular employee create a fourth type of problem when they act out their hostility or amuse themselves at the resented employee's expense. Examples include men who resent the presence of a woman in a mostly male workplace, and white employees who resent the presence of a black employee in a mostly white workplace.

We could conclude that, if employees are having personal problems, it is nobody's business but their own. In the 1970s and early 1980s, before some forms of sexual harassment were widely considered to be a violation of the law, many judges characterized abusive sexual demands by supervisors as "personality conflicts" and "relationships gone bad." The fact that many relationships end happily leads some people to say that employers and the courts should let people resolve these problems themselves. Most of us know someone who has experienced unacceptable behavior at work and survived the situation without serious repercussions.

There is nothing new about men imposing unwanted social or sexual attention upon women. There is also nothing new about women having to put up with sexual attention to keep their jobs, or even sometimes using sex to obtain benefits they could not otherwise obtain. There is also nothing new about people in authority, whether men or women, misusing their authority for personal gain.

Major changes in the law and in the culture of the workplace over the last five decades have required us to change our views of situations at work that have traditionally been considered to be personal issues. First, and most important, the law has changed dramatically. Federal, state, and local laws now protect workers from discrimination based on sex, race, religion, disability, and other characteristics. These laws are intended to remove obstacles to employment for our nation's workers. These laws interfere with how employers run their businesses and treat their employees in areas where they once had nearly complete freedom. The law also makes employers responsible for their employees' working conditions in ways that they have never before been responsible.

The second change is the demographic makeup of the American workplace. Women are now nearly one in every two American workers. This demographic shift is having a major impact on the social climate and the social reality in American workplaces.

The major law prohibiting unlawful discrimination in employment is Title VII of the Civil Rights Act of 1964 (commonly referred to as Title VII). Title VII prohibits employers from discriminating against employees, or treating them differently, based on race, color, religion, sex, or national origin. Title VII, together with the state and local laws that are modeled after it, granted workers significant new rights. Because women and ethnic racial groups were traditionally excluded from many employment opportunities, women and minority workers stood to gain the most from Title VII. Another important law enacted one year earlier, the Equal Pay Act of 1963, prohibits paying men and women different wages for jobs that require equal skill, effort, and responsibility, unless the difference in pay is based on a factor other than sex.

Today, an employer who treats women differently than men, simply because they are female, is violating the law. For example, before Title VII and the Equal Pay Act of 1963 became law, an employer could lawfully refuse to hire a woman, or hire her at a lower salary than a man received for doing the same work, because she was female. Now, an employer also violates the law if he or she treats a woman differently than a man because she is pregnant, married, has young children, is not attractive enough, cannot type, or for any other reason.

Title VII also covers working conditions and how workers are treated. If women have to endure different working conditions than are imposed on men, the employer can be held responsible for allowing discriminatory working conditions to exist. Under Title VII, social or sexual behavior directed toward an employee because of her or his sex or gender creates discriminatory working conditions if the behavior affects the employee's job.

Laws prohibiting sexual harassment define sexual harassment as "unwanted" sexual behavior that affects an employee's experience of the workplace in certain defined ways. When unwanted sexual behavior affects working conditions, it becomes an obstacle to employment based on the employee's sex.

Different treatment of women, sometimes demeaning and derogatory treatment, is deeply ingrained in our culture. Traditionally, how we speak to, treat, and regard women has been considered to be within the arena of private behavior. The need to comply with Title VII and other antidiscrimination laws has caused significant shifts in American workplace practices, priorities, behavior, values, sensibilities, and language.

We resist change, but the resistance to change in the area of discrimination, particularly in the area of sex discrimination and sexual harassment, has been different.

The law of sexual harassment attempts to regulate behavior that many people tend to consider to be beyond the reach of the law. Some employees have reacted with confusion, resentment, resistance, and fear. Like the engineer who wants to find women to date, men want to know: How can the law say I can't ask a woman for a date? Where do you draw the line? How far can I go? Like Joan, who was shocked by her boss's invitation to view a pornographic movie, women want to know: What can I do when my supervisor makes inappropriate advances?

Behaviors that have long been out of reach of laws and regulation are suddenly the subject of million-dollar lawsuits. Today, American businesses are reeling from the costs of unchecked sexual behavior in the workplace. Laws prohibiting sexual harassment have received varied reactions. Some employers now require employees to sign a disclosure statement when they intend to enter a sexual relationship. Other employers prohibit their employees from engaging in sexual or romantic relationships during their employment with nonfraternization policies. Under so-called "zero tolerance" policies, employers impose maximum penalties for all violations of their antifraternization and sexual harassment policies. Some men fear that complimenting a woman's hairstyle or approaching her socially in any way will jeopardize their jobs.

At the same time, a dramatic increase in the number of working women is altering the social experience of the American workplace. At an earlier time in our country's history, many women (though certainly not all) could simply walk away from an unacceptable situation because their salary was supplemental, and not the primary income in the household.

Now, women have much more to lose if they walk away. As more women enter the workforce, fewer of them stay at home under the protection of their families until they marry. And more married women than ever before are working outside the home. The presence of larger numbers of women tends to give individual women greater confidence to complain about unacceptable behaviors at work.

In many sectors of the economy, women have moved into positions of power and influence in which they can voice the concerns of women workers. Women are now working in nontraditional fields and positions from which they were previously excluded, such as law, medicine, finance, journalism, and construction. Women can now be found on corporate boards, in chief executive offices, among business owners, and in supervisory positions. The women's movement gives a public voice to concerns of working women, making it difficult for lawmakers and employers to ignore inequities.

Ironically, women in positions of supervisory power are able to impose unwanted and offensive behavior on their male and female subordinates just as men in supervisory positions are able to do. Women supervisors can threaten or imply the loss of a job, job benefits, or career advancement. This phenomenon allows female supervisors to sexually harass men. Even though studies show that the majority of workers who experience sexual harassment on the job are female, men can be sexually harassed. Anyone who works for someone else can be sexually harassed.

We could end sexual harassment quickly and easily if we all applied three simple rules that we all should have learned as children:

1. Leave anyone alone who doesn't want to play.
2. Don't be mean.
3. Don't pick on little kids.

These are great rules, but they are not always easy to apply in practice.

Rule Number One, "Leave anyone alone who doesn't want to play," should be an easy rule to follow. Rule Number One boils down to listening to other people and complying with their wishes. If you hear anything other that an unambiguous welcoming signal, then you cease and desist. Following Rule Number One comes with a couple of wrinkles: You have to be interested in the other person's wishes, and the other person has to say whether he or she wants to play.

Unfortunately, people aren't always direct about whether they want to play. Sometimes they don't want to "rock the boat," hurt someone's feelings, or displease someone. Sometimes, they don't know whether they want to play. They are equivocal; they don't say yes or no. They say something that can be misinterpreted or taken either way. Sometimes, they say no and it is heard as yes. Of course, there are also people who don't take no for an answer even if it is a clear, unmistakable no.

Rule Number Two, "Don't be mean," can be even more difficult to apply. Most of us are not mean to others on purpose. However, some of us can be very mean. We can hurt, offend, intimidate, and upset other people. Sometimes, we do it intentionally. Often, we don't notice or care about our impact on other people. Some people are mean, believing they have no control over themselves. Under sexual harassment law, the impact or effect of behavior is just as important as the purpose of the behavior. I have often heard people accused of sexually harassing a coworker say, "I didn't mean anything by it; I was just kidding around." The intentions don't matter if the effect of the behavior is to offend, intimidate, or humiliate the other person.

The humiliated employee is sometimes reluctant to say anything. (See Rule Number One.) He or she is stunned, hurt, embarrassed, and completely disbelieving that anyone could treat another person in that manner. The offending coworker, in his or her own world, thinks the joke was funny or his or her offer tempting. He or she considers the rejecting person to be "super sensitive," "a prude," or "in a bad mood today." In the sexual harassment arena, it doesn't matter that the behavior was unintentional. The toughest part of applying Rule Number Two is that mean is in the eye of the beholder.

Rule Number Three, "Don't pick on little kids," is probably the toughest of the three rules to apply in real life. Sexual harassment is less about sex than it is about power. Nearly one in every two harassers is the direct supervisor of the person he or she is harassing. Abuses of power by supervisors are the most egregious form of sexual harassment and among the most difficult to address. Most supervisors take their roles very seriously and avoid using their power in inappropriate ways. Nevertheless, power is tempting, and people abuse power. Supervisors and people who abuse power to get what they want and to dominate others are the minority. This minority is the subject of most sexual harassment lawsuits. Of course, supervisors and managers are not the only ones who exercise power in the workplace. Groups and individuals also exert power in the workplace environment. In Chapters 4, 5, and 13, we will address abuses of power more expansively.

Consider the case of the female employee who had sexual intercourse with her boss approximately 50 times during four years because she was afraid she would lose her job. In court, the employer argued that she had engaged in sexual relations voluntarily. According to the Supreme Court, the question is not whether her conduct was voluntary, but whether the boss's conduct was welcome.

In that case, the boss was clearly interested in getting what he wanted (sex with his female subordinate). Without question, anyone who asks another for sex is interested in a yes answer and listens for anything that can be interpreted as yes. The law of sexual harassment requires that the speaker listen equally closely for no or for behavior that indicates the absence of yes. Supervisors are big kids. When big kids pretend that little kids are free to say no to them, they are kidding themselves. That's why little kids are in such a hurry to be big kids, so they can protect themselves from the big kids.

There are two main points here:

1. In virtually every case, it is unrealistic and dangerous to expect a subordinate to feel free to accept or reject a supervisor's sexual behavior.

2. Someone has to make sure that supervisors, whether they are hopeful, stupid, or predatory, are not taking advantage of employees.

Some little kids lie about having been picked on. We have all probably been in trouble at one time or another when someone said we picked on them but we didn't. Men fear being falsely accused of sexually harassing a fellow worker. This can and does happen. It is a real concern we will address in Chapters 8, 9, and 11.

We have all also probably experienced not being believed by the grown-ups when we complained that another kid picked on us. Women are afraid they won't be believed if they complain about sexual harassment. This is another real concern we will address in Chapters 7, 9, and 11.

Sexual harassment occurs in the larger context of work and work relationships. Sexual harassment also occurs against the background of how we expect coworkers and organizations to respond, based on our past experiences. How we address, respond to, and understand social/sexual relations and sexual harassment in the workplace is affected by the existing culture at work. Creating healthy work relationships and healthy work environments will require altering well-established power relationships. Sexual harassment will be simpler to address, though not necessarily easy to address, in a respectful, communicative workplace in which the three rules are generally followed. Addressing sexual harassment will be more difficult in a workplace where supervisors hold little respect for their subordinates and are encouraged or tolerated in following their personal agendas. As we will see in the remaining chapters of Part I, the shift has already begun.

Most people become aware of sexual harassment from two sources: the news and situations at their workplace. Many Americans were first exposed to the issue in 1991 when Anita Hill accused Clarence Thomas of sexually harassing her years earlier when they both worked for a government agency. Professor Hill's supporters wore "I believe Anita" T-shirts that highlighted two critical issues that are usually present in sexual harassment cases: It is difficult to know who is telling the truth, and the accuser is sometimes both disbelieved and punished for bringing the accusation. The hearings polarized the country. On one side were those who believed Professor Hill's accusations and were outraged by the treatment she received from the Senate Committee. On the other side were those who believed she was a vengeful, scorned woman, as Committee Chair Orrin Hatch described her, who should not be taken seriously because she had waited 10 years to tell her story.

In 1998, President Bill Clinton was the subject of a sexual harassment lawsuit brought by Paula Jones. In addition, Special Prosecutor Kenneth Starr's lurid report revealed that the President had engaged in a sexual relationship with White House intern Monica Lewinsky inside the Oval Office. President Clinton's credibility became the subject of heated national debate and the central issue of his impeachment trial.

In August of 2004, New Jersey Governor Jim McGreevey shocked constituents when he announced he would resign the governorship because he had been involved in a consensual sexual relationship with a male employee, stating that he feared an involuntary disclosure would have a negative impact on the Office of the Governor. A few days later, the male employee publicly charged that Governor McGreevey had sexually harassed him. Although no lawsuit has been filed, the employee said that the governor had used his considerable power to force him to engage in sex.

These sensational, high profile cases have been helpful in raising the public's awareness of sexual harassment, but they encourage a distorted view of the nature and frequency of sexual harassment in workplaces across the nation. Government and private surveys, studies, and reports show that sexual harassment is common.

Sexual harassment is common, and it affects a significant number of American workers. In 2003, the Equal Employment Opportunity Commission (the federal agency that enforces Title VII) and state and local enforcement agencies received 13,566 sexual harassment complaints, which represents a 15 percent increase over the number of sexual harassment complaints received a decade earlier. Men filed 15 percent of the complaints, compared to nine percent in 1993. The number of men who complained they were sexually harassed by a female supervisor tripled in recent years. Two thirds of those responding to a national survey said they had experienced sexual harassment on the job. Between 40 percent and 50 percent of those who responded to a survey of service and industrial workers said they had experienced sexual harassment, but took no action in response. Fully 62 percent of businesses consider sexual harassment to be a significant workplace issue. Most employers report that they conduct sexual harassment training for their employees, and virtually all employers have a written sexual harassment policy.

Yet the law remains difficult to understand, and the rules can be difficult to apply in practice. When survey respondents say they have been sexually harassed, some of them were sexually assaulted, some lost job benefits because they resisted a supervisor's sexual demands, and others received offensive e-mail. With such a broad array of behaviors, workers are confused about what is prohibited and what is allowed.

In addition, the definition of sexual harassment appears to be continually changing. We rely on the courts to interpret laws passed by the legislatures. Every time a court issues a decision on a sexual harassment case, the law of sexual harassment can change. These changes can be barely notice-able or major. The highest court in the United States is the Supreme Court, whose decisions influence the decisions of every other court. From 1964, when Title VII (the nation's first comprehensive fair employment law) was passed, until 1998, the U.S. Supreme Court issued two decisions on sexual harassment. For years, courts and lawyers were guided by these two decisions. During this time state courts and lower federal courts issued numerous decisions, but the Supreme Court had been curiously silent in the area of sexual harassment.

Then, in June of 1998, the Supreme Court issued three important decisions on sexual harassment, sending sexual harassment lawyers back to their drawing boards. Both plain-tiffs' and defense lawyers had to rethink advice they'd been giving their clients for years. One case involved a group of male workers on an oil rig off the coast of Texas who touched, grabbed, and threatened to rape a gay male coworker. An-other case involved the complaints of female lifeguards em-ployed by the City of Boca Raton, Florida, whose male supervisors regularly grabbed them in sexual manner and de-manded sex as a condition of keeping their jobs. The third case involved a supervisor at Burlington Industries who threat-ened an employee with negative consequences if she resisted his continual sexual behavior. The Court made big news in the world of sexual harassment law by ruling:

- Men can harass other men, even if there is no actual sexual interest;

- An employer may be held legally and financially responsible when a supervisor sexually harasses an employee, even if the employee never reported the sexual harassment;

- Employers can avoid being legally and financially responsible for sexual harassment of their employees by showing they have in place an effective sexual harassment policy, procedure, and training; and

- Employers have no defense when an employee loses tangible job benefits as the result of being sexually harassed by a supervisor.

This was very big news for lawyers and judges. Clients now pay big fees for advice on how to protect themselves in light of the new rules. However, the typical employee, small business owner, or supervisor is not going to read a 100-page Supreme Court opinion. They aren't going to consult a lawyer about every situation at work that might become sexually charged. Regular people need a plain English translation of the law, how it applies to them, and what it requires them to do in situations they face every day.

This book isn't a substitute for good legal advice. It will give you an edge in terms of what to look for, how to prevent problems, how to react on the spot, and, if necessary, when to call a lawyer. If you have to call a lawyer, you'll have a good idea why you called and what to ask. When the lawyers arrive, they will take over. I want you to have the information, skills, and power to deal effectively with sexually charged situations before somebody calls a lawyer.

2

Updating the Greek Tragedy

The first problem I faced when I started to write this book was how to write it so that anyone could relate to what I was saying and take away something useful. How could I write so that men and women can both hear what I have to say? The conversation around sexual harassment isn't so much a conversation as it is a debate between two points of view: the woman's point of view and the man's point of view. One person is the victim and the other person is the villain. Those two points of view were so deeply ingrained in my thinking that anything I wrote automatically expressed my point of view as a woman. At every turn, I found myself protecting and defending the victim or castigating and punishing the villain. I found myself thinking, "If only men would change, this whole problem would go away." I was trapped inside a cultural debate. If I was trapped in my own point of view, after 30 years of experience in this area, anyone reading my book would also have his or her own point of view.

I was committed to writing a book that gave anyone who read it a new view of what is possible in how men and women relate in the workplace. How do I write a book that a man can read without being called a harasser or being made to feel like a villain? How do I write a book a woman can read without being called a victim? Most men are not sexual harassers. Some men sexually harass because they don't know the rules or don't appreciate the effect of their behavior on others, while others harass because they just don't care about their impact on others. The vast majority of men respect the women with whom they work and follow the law. I became convinced that women needed to start gaining personal power in the workplace. To cast them as the victims would be to treat them as powerless and needing to be rescued from dominating and abusive men.

How could I write so that an employer can get as much from this book as an employee? How could I make it relevant to both a supervisor and a subordinate? Employees are concerned about how to protect themselves from harassment, accusations, and the possible consequences of a false accusation. Supervisors are concerned about what to do when someone complains she has been sexually harassed. Employers are concerned about being sued by their employees. Is it possible to speak to the concerns of all these affected groups?

Women can harass men. Men can harass other men. Women can harass other women. Wherever one person is in a position of power over someone else, sexual harassment can happen. The "woman's" point of view loses relevance when both people are the same sex. The lines of demarcation between victims and villains are so deeply ingrained in our attitudes that we must cast one person in the role of the victim in order to grasp the story. Inside the woman's point of view, the victim of the harassment, the one in the traditional woman's role, is the victim. On one side, the victim is the receiver of the harassment. On the other side, the victim is the accused. Given these two seemingly irreconcilable points of view, creating a universally accessible way of speaking about sexual harassment seemed impossible.

Whatever I wrote would alienate someone. I was willing to alienate those who don't agree with what I have to say. But I was not willing to alienate people just because I don't know how to speak to them.

In the background, coloring everything, are characterizations of whole groups of people as villains. The woman's point of view characterizes men as selfish, abusive, uncaring villains. The man's point of view characterizes women as unreasonable, oversensitive, vindictive villains. Both points of view characterize supervisors as arrogant, controlling villains. Both points of view characterize supervisors as either gullible, over-reactive, judgmental, or uncaring villains.

In the course of my unscientific research, I spoke to hundreds of people. I found I could say I was writing a book on sexual harassment, then listen. The subject was already provocative, and I discovered a great deal.

I spoke to men from many different backgrounds and walks of life: doctors, lawyers, teachers, office workers, businessmen, security guards, doormen, handymen, taxi drivers, truck drivers, construction workers, laborers, and janitorial workers. Every man I spoke to had a question or comment about how the law of sexual harassment works. Some men sought to justify their own inappropriate behaviors or to argue that the laws prohibiting sexual harassment make no sense. For the most part, however, all the men with whom I spoke had questions about what the law really required and expressed a genuine desire to avoid sexually harassing the women with whom they work. All the men I spoke to were skeptical about whether I was interested in what they had to say.

Some men had experienced being sexually harassed. Some had been accused of sexually harassing someone and felt powerless to defend themselves. Others knew women supervisors who sexually exploited the men who worked for them and wanted me to reassure them that the laws prohibiting sexual harassment also protected men. Some of the stories they told me were shocking. An expert in sexual harassment law with more than 30 years of legal experience, I thought I'd heard everything. I hadn't. At a recent social gathering, several men who work for a large government agency said of a female supervisor, "If you want to be promoted, you have to 'stretch her out.'" It was common knowledge, they disclosed, that the supervisor required her male subordinates to have sex with her in order to advance in their careers.

Every woman to whom I spoke told me a story of being sexually harassed at work. Their stories were different, and they dealt with the problem in different ways. It struck me, however, that every women had a story. Many older women who were no longer working told me stories of sexual aggression by supervisors that occurred long before there were laws prohibiting sexual harassment. Some had never before told their experiences to anyone. Younger women who had recently entered the workforce told me they had come to expect inappropriate sexual behavior from their colleagues and that their only choices are to either to endure the behavior or to find another job.

Among the people I spoke to were those who were convinced they wouldn't be believed if they reported that they were sexually harassed. This wasn't surprising, because I had encountered many women who were afraid to report incidents of sexual harassment for just this reason. In addition, the literature demonstrates clearly that many women do not report the harassment because they fear they won't be believed. I was surprised to hear from several men who believed they had been sexually harassed on the job, but feared they would be disbelieved, or worse, ridiculed for reporting the problem.

Another group I encountered were men convinced there is nothing they can do to defend themselves if they are accused of sexual harassment. These men tended to be service workers and blue-collar workers who regularly encounter female customers. Building workers (doormen, porters, and handymen), as well as repairmen said they would lose their jobs immediately if they were accused of approaching a tenant or homeowner sexually. Many of them knew other male service workers who had been accused of sexually inappropriate behavior and then summarily dismissed with no opportunity to defend themselves.

I still had the problem of finding a voice that men and women, supervisors and subordinates, accuser and accused, could hear, relate to, and learn from without being excluded. I found the answer in two places. The first place was my attitude toward my audience. I pictured all these people reading my words, and I started to notice that what I thought about people influenced what I wrote. Some people, I thought, wouldn't "get it." Others, I thought, needed to be set straight. The second place was the language I was using. The words I wrote could exclude people. When I write, am I creating a class of villains or a class of victims? Am I excoriating or pacifying? It became clear that the language that was available to me was insufficient for the book I wanted to write. The language in which we speak of sexual harassment is, itself, divisive and exclusionary. I had to invent a new point of view, one that includes all the existing points of view, but aligns with none of them. I had to invent a new language, one that was understandable to English-speakers, but a language that allowed me to speak to everyone.

Let me give an example of the dilemma. I wanted to offer my readers new possibilities for working together that would allow them to recognize sexually charged or sexually abusive situations and to act consciously and effectively. Most people who find themselves in situations involving sexual harassment experience it as a complete surprise. One day, they are doing what they do every day. The next day, they wake up into a nightmare. A coworker has done something very disturbing, and they don't know what to do about it, or someone has accused them of engaging in sexually harassing behavior. Suddenly they are in trouble and trying to survive the situation. Questions that were never that important are now on the front burner: Is this sexual harassment? What can I do? Can anything be done? Is someone going to be fired? Am I going to be fired?

These were the most common questions I encountered. Many people, including a well-known journalist I spoke with, said that sexual harassment is hard to understand because the rules keep changing. I wanted to provide a useful, universally applicable, plain English definition that would remain useful, even when the rules change. I wanted to enable people to have nightmarish situations turn out differently.

Just stating the situation requires naming the players. Conventional language calls the person who is experiencing the behavior the victim, typically a woman. Conventional language calls the person who is being accused the harasser, who is typically a man. Those terms don't work. For one thing, if we are asking whether the behavior is sexual harassment, it begs the question to refer to the behavior as sexual harassment. It is, at best, premature to say there is a victim. We certainly don't have a harasser, at least not yet. We have someone who believes something inappropriate happened. We have someone who may or may not have done something unlawful. Even referring to those involved as she and he invokes the male villain vs. the female victim cultural debate. I needed a new language just to describe what happened.

Traditional Roles	
Employer	(Innocent Bystanders)
Victim	Harasser

After a lot of soul searching, I realized something extraordinary. I took the case of a female employee, before anything happens. Will she be the one making the accusation, the one being accused, the one to whom the complaint is made, or the one who ultimately decides how the situation will be resolved? The answer to this question was the first of a series of realizations that made it possible for me to write the book. She could be in any of these roles. Clearly, she could be the one making the accusation or deciding what to do about disturbing behavior. Whether she is a line employee, a supervisor, a manager, or an executive, she can be sexually harassed. She also could be the one accused of sexually harassing another employee. Most people understand that, as a supervisor, she can harass a subordinate. She can also harass a coworker who is on her level in the organization. This involves a concept known as hostile environment harassment, the gray area of the law. She could be the one to whom the complaint is made, by virtue of her supervisory position or her role as the person in the organization to whom complaints are to be made. She could be the one assigned to investigate a complaint. She could be the business owner or other person who must decide what action the organization will take. My hypothetical female employee could be in any one of these roles. The role she is in can't be determined until something happens. Thus, my first realization was that I don't know what role the reader is in, and the reader might not know what role he or she might be called upon to play.

The same thing is true for the hypothetical male employee. He could also find himself in any of the roles. As a line employee, a supervisor, a manager, or an executive, he could be sexually harassed. He could be the one who experiences inappropriate behavior and is deciding what to do about it. He could be the one accused of sexually harassing another employee, whether a subordinate or a coworker on his level in the organization. He could certainly be the person to whom a complaint has been made or the person who has been designated in the organization to receive and/or investigate complaints. He could be the business owner or other person who must decide what action the organization will take. The role my hypothetical male employee is playing can't be determined until something happens.

At first, it was disorienting to realize that I couldn't know which role the reader would be playing, as he or she read the book. Then, it was freeing. If the reader could be playing any role, then perhaps the reader can appreciate the point of view and experience of someone in another role. Perhaps.

This new all-inclusive perspective was fleeting. I wrote one sentence, and it was gone. I had to stand up, walk around, get some fresh air, and write another sentence. I was inventing a new perspective as I wrote. Even if I could maintain this new perspective, could I expect my reader to stay with me? Was it too much to ask?

I was skeptical about whether this new view could work, in all situations. Is it true than anyone can be sexually harassed? I decided to test my theory. During this critical creative period, I had dinner with a friend who had just accepted the presidency at a private college. This was, in part, a dinner celebrating his big promotion. As had become my custom, I mentioned I was writing a book on sexual harassment. I listened to what he had to say. I commented that anyone could be sexually harassed.

He said, "Yes, I think we have a good policy and training for the students, faculty, and staff. Thank goodness, I don't have to worry about that sort of thing personally."

I said, "I'm not kidding. You could be sexually harassed, even at your lofty position. I assume you accepted this job on the assurances and promises of members of the Board of Trustees that they will support certain initiatives that are important to you. I'm sure you made requests and they promised you a lot of money for what you want to accomplish for the college."

He said, "That's a fair assumption."

I continued, "Let's assume that, upon your arrival at the new job, one of your board members, the key source of the funds you are expecting and the principal source of private financing for the college, tells you that she supported you for the job, not just because of your credentials, but also because you are so cute and sexy. She says that, if you want her to come through with the money, you have to have sex with her. Otherwise, all bets are off."

My friend was so stunned that he almost dropped his drink. I apologized for upsetting him and explained that this is how many instances of sexual harassment occur. I asked what he would do. He said it was so far outside anything he had considered possible that he had no idea what he would do. He also protested that it would never happen. I asked him to play along for the sake of my project. It was clear to him that no one would believe him if he tried to stop the exploitation, and that, given the board member's relative power, he would lose out if he tried to fight her. He saw his obvious options: submit to her demand, stay and lose the funds, or give up the job. None of these options was satisfactory. In the end, my friend agreed that, if this is what it is like to experience sexual harassment on the job, new tools are needed.

My next task was to step fully into the new perspective, both managing and embracing my own point of view. I also had to invent a new language for speaking about sexual harassment.

The Greek Tragedy
In the summer of 1982, I presented my first training workshops on sexual harassment for corporate employees. In those

days, I had to spend the first 30 minutes of the workshop convincing the participants that sexual harassment existed and that it concerned them. In each workshop, a male workshop participant always asked, "Is this really a problem? Why do I have to spend my time on something that might not really be happening?" Statistics from two published studies and a courageous female participant's story typically convinced the men that this was a real issue.

I don't have to do that anymore. Now, the pendulum has swung in the other direction. Everyone has at least heard of sexual harassment, and everyone knows that when someone says the words "sexual harassment," it means trouble for someone else. Situations that involve or might involve sexual harassment take on the drama of a Greek tragedy. Whenever we hear about a situation that involves sexual harassment, we become instantly caught up in the high drama.

Tragic Roles	
Omnipotent God	The Chorus
Antagonist	Protagonist

Every Greek tragedy has certain elements and follows a predictable formula. The central players in the Greek tragedy are the antagonist and the protagonist. There are always an antagonist and protagonist, and we always want to know who they are. We need to know who they are, in order to understand the story and know whom to support. The other players in the Greek tragedy are the all-powerful, mythical god, the mythical god's favorite mortal, and the chorus. The omnipotent god can be kind or angry. The omnipotent god's role is to determine the outcome. The chorus observes the actions of the other players and tells the story.

The antagonist

The antagonist is the bad guy, the one who is causing the problem. The antagonist is the one who is in the wrong, without whom everyone else would be carrying on as usual, without the problem. Without the antagonist and the problem, there would be no drama.

Depending on your point of view, the antagonist can be the sexual harasser—the abusive, inconsiderate, overpowering, or predatory supervisor or coworker—or the antagonist can be the unreasonable, oversensitive, or vindictive person who is causing the problem for the poor person who didn't do anything wrong. The identity of the antagonist is determined by your point of view.

The protagonist

The protagonist is the good guy, the one who is being attacked or exploited. You need to know who the protagonist is so you can root for him or her. The protagonist is the one with the problem, or the victim. Without the protagonist's problem, there would be no drama. The protagonist is usually the innocent, hardworking person who has to put up with the unwanted sexual attention of a harasser. The protagonist can also be the poor unsuspecting person who didn't do anything wrong. It depends on your point of view. It's easy to identify the protagonist. The protagonist is the one you relate to and for whom you feel sorry. The protagonist is the one your gut tells you should win in the end.

The omnipotent god

The next player is the angry or helpful omnipotent god. In the ancient Greek tragedies, the omnipotent god is the all-powerful mythical figure who protects the protagonist, punishes the antagonist, and controls how the story will turn out. Everyone waits for the decision of the omnipotent god to know the outcome. In the sexual harassment scenario, the omnipotent god is the executive or the business owner, whoever makes the final decision on what will be done after someone sexually harasses someone else. The omnipotent god makes decisions based on factors that the other players don't understand, and he or she tends to make all or nothing decisions. You either win with the omnipotent god or you lose. Losing with the omnipotent god means being exiled, killed, abandoned, or ruined. The omnipotent god is all-powerful but not all knowing. This player can be angry or kind. It depends on your point of view.

The chorus

We rarely notice the final group of players, the chorus. In the ancient Greek tragedies, the chorus is always on stage. Sometimes they are in the shadows, but they are always there. The chorus observes the other players, judges the other players, predicts what will happen to them, warns of impending doom, spreads rumors, decides whether things are going well or badly, and tells the lessons learned. The chorus does all this with no apparent involvement in the actual events. In the sexual harassment scenario, they are the coworkers who talk among themselves and spread the story. They appear to be doing nothing, and we believe they have no effect on the action and the outcome. At work, we typically call them innocent bystanders.

Now that we have introduced the players, we can start to see how the drama of sexual harassment plays out in the workplace. The antagonist and the protagonist set the scene. One is a good guy, and the other is the bad guy. The omnipotent god decides what will happen in the end, inflicting an extreme result on one of the two key players. The chorus observes and tells the story. In the end, the situation turns out tragically for someone (or for everyone).

Action–Based Roles

Like the Greek tragedies, sexual harassment scenarios tend to end badly for one or all of the players. The person being harassed quits or is left in an untenable situation; the accused person loses his job or suffers some other form of discipline; and the employer pays a hefty judgment or settlement after a lawsuit.

It doesn't have to go that way. People who find themselves confronting possible sexual harassment can take action to create another kind of outcome, one that doesn't have to be tragic. I am not suggesting that it is possible in all instances. Sometimes, people who sexually harass do not respond to training and education, do not care about the effect of their actions on others, and cannot be stopped without harsh discipline. Sometimes people make false accusations and cause damage. Yet these are not the typical case. In nearly every case, it doesn't have to end badly.

In the usual sexual harassment scenario, the conventional language requires us to know, in advance, who is right and who is wrong, just to describe what happened. As we explore the definition of sexual harassment and ask whether particular situations involve sexual harassment, we need to reserve judgment. Some situations don't involve sexual harassment at all. The conventional language doesn't allow us to reach that conclusion. We are stuck with terms such as "victim," "harasser," "accuser," and "accused." When we need to suspend our judgment, these terms won't serve our purpose. Using these terms actually thwarts our purpose. For example, consider the problem faced by a woman who has experienced a disturbing encounter with a coworker and doesn't know what to do about it. If we call her the victim, we have prejudged whether she was sexually harassed. If we call the coworker the harasser, we have prejudged his actions. If we call them the accused and the accuser, we create an adversarial situation. If there is no accusation, these terms are inaccurate. Conventional language doesn't serve our purpose.

In my 21 years of investigating sexual harassment complaints for two major organizations, my job required suspending my judgment about what happened until after I had collected all the available testimony and evidence. It wasn't always easy, especially when the person making the complaint appeared to be credible or the alleged facts were unusual. Eventually, I realized that I couldn't avoid having a premature opinion. I learned how to set aside my opinions, evaluate the facts, and come to a conclusion. Unless I witnessed the events, I couldn't possibly know what happened. My job was to conclude what probably happened and to recommend actions to the decision-maker. The best I could do was to be reasonably certain about what happened.

Repeatedly, I watched as organizations became polarized and people took sides, protected their friends, campaigned for or against the perceived victim, and campaigned for or against the perceived harasser. In a surprising number of cases, both parties agreed on what happened. The only disagreement was whether the actions could be called sexual harassment, or whether the sexual harassment was serious enough to warrant disciplinary action.

The first step in altering the outcome is to alter the language that reflects premature judgment. We need language that eliminates judgment. We have to take the notion of good guys and bad guys out of the equation. Altering our language will alter how we see the events and the players.

The terms we typically use give us our perspective and outlook. For example, when we say victim, we assume that the person has been victimized and that he or she is powerless. Likewise, when we say harasser, we assume that the harasser has, indeed, sexually harassed the victim. This is not to say that we should disbelieve the victim. It is merely to say that the term "victim" is so loaded and so judgmental as to prejudge the desired outcome. The harasser must be punished or banished. The terms we use have us choose sides. They require those who side with the harasser to attack the victim in order to protect the harasser.

When the actual events occur, or when someone complains that she or he has been sexually harassed, there is often an opportunity to turn events around and create mutual understanding and respect. This is possible only if we reserve judgment and shift our perspective. We will start by calling the key players by new names.

Action-Based Roles	
Responsible Supervisor	Active Observer
Target	Actor

Target

The term "target," instead of victim, represents the person toward whom behavior is directed. It is neutral, nonjudgmental, and analytical. This will help eliminate the notion of a good guy or a bad guy. The target is the person toward whom the action in question was directed, or the target of the action.

Actor

The term, "actor," instead of "harasser" or "accused," is also neutral and nonjudgmental. It refers to the person whose actions are in question. We can more easily assess the behavior if we call that person by a name other than harasser or accused. The actor is neither a good guy nor a bad guy. He or she is the one who acted.

Responsible supervisor

In the sexual harassment scenario, "employer" is a legal term. It refers to the person or the corporation that is responsible for enforcing the law. The employer is also the one who pays the settlement or verdict in a lawsuit. While some employers are individual business owners, most employers are corporations or partnerships.

The problem with speaking about corporations and companies is they don't really exist, not in the sense that we can see them or talk to them. Unless you are writing a legal document, the term "employer" isn't a practical term. In the real world, the employer acts through agents, real people who make decisions and interact with the employees. In the real world, the employer's responsibilities belong to real people who have legal obligations, rather than to an impersonal, conceptual employer.

There is a real person who is responsible for acting on behalf of the employer in response to possible sexual harassment and to prevent sexual harassment in the particular workplace. In a practical sense, the employer is a person we can see, talk to, and find in a telephone book. Because this is intended to be a practical discussion, we'll avoid using the term "employer."

In the real world, someone is responsible for monitoring, investigating, and remedying discrimination in a particular situation. It is someone's job to receive reports of possible sexual harassment, to determine whether someone was sexually harassed, or to take action if unlawful harassment has occurred. We'll call that person the "responsible supervisor." This person has the power and the opportunity to act when a possible situation involving sexual harassment comes to his or her attention. The responsible supervisor has a critical role.

Active observers

Finally, there are the coworkers. In the typical sexual harassment scenario, we call them innocent bystanders. They are the ones who talk about what happened, console one side or the other, and send e-mails with the latest news. They often have critical knowledge that can support a fair resolution. Most important, they watch silently, measuring the parties' behavior against their own standards. We pretend they aren't involved, when clearly they are. We'll call them the "active observers". The active observers do not have legal obligations, but we'll explore how their seemingly innocent behavior influences the events and the ultimate outcome. They can often act to alter the course of events. For now, we'll ask: Why are they important? What could they do? As we will see, the active observers play a critical role.

We now have new names, or action-based roles, for the players: target, actor, responsible supervisor, and active observer. These action-based roles are the first step toward identifying actions the players can take to alter the predictable course of events. Now we can define sexual harassment and take a new look at what happens when an incident of possible sexual harassment occurs.

What Is Sexual Harassment?

When the Congress enacted Title VII of the Civil Rights Act of 1964, it also created the Equal Employment Opportunity Commission (EEOC). The EEOC is the federal agency that investigates employees' complaints of employment discrimination and has the authority to sue employers on behalf of the federal government to correct discriminatory practices that affect individual employees or groups of employees. The EEOC also provides guidelines and advice to employers and employees about their rights and responsibilities under Title VII. In 1980, the EEOC issued a definition of sexual harassment.

The EEOC's definition is commonly accepted and appears in most state and local laws, court decisions, and employers' sexual harassment policies:

• • •

Unwelcome sexual advances, requests for sexual favors, or other verbal or physical conduct of a sexual nature, constitute sexual harassment when:

1) submission to such conduct is made either explicitly or implicitly a term or condition of an individual's employment, or

2) submission to or rejection of such conduct by an individual is used as the basis for employment decisions affecting such individual, or

3) such conduct has the purpose or effect of unreasonably interfering with an individual's work performance or creating an intimidating, hostile, or offensive work environment.

• • •

Plainly stated, sexual harassment happens when there is unwanted sex-related behavior, plus a particular kind of impact on an employee, specifically:

- The employee rejects the unwanted behavior and loses a job offer, a job, or other tangible job benefits;

- The employee puts up with the unwanted behavior in order to get a job, to keep a job or to get some other tangible job benefit; or

- The intention or the result of the unwanted sexual behavior is that the employee's work performance suffers or the employee experiences the workplace as offensive, intimidating, or hostile.

Sexual harassment always involves four elements. First, there must be an action, such as the actor putting his arms around the target. The action can be physical, verbal, or visual. Second, the action must be unwelcome or unwanted in the target's view. Third, the action must be sexual or sex-related and based on the target's sex or gender. Fourth, there has to be a tangible economic impact on the target or a severely negative impact on the target's work performance or work environment.

There are two types of sexual harassment, *quid pro quo* **harassment** and **hostile environment harassment.** Most people understand *quid pro quo* harassment as sex in direct exchange for employment benefits. Mary applies for a job and Tom, the interviewer, tells her she will get the job if she has sex with him. If Mary does not welcome Tom's behavior, has sex with him, and gets the job, it is sexual harassment. If Mary refuses to have sex and does not get the job, it is sexual harassment.

In *quid pro quo* harassment, the supervisor's demand does not have to be direct. It can be implied by touching or suggestive comments. If the target loses a tangible economic benefit as the result of accepting or rejecting the actor's demand, the behavior, the sexual nature of the behavior, the fact that the behavior is unwanted, and the loss, together, are sexual harassment. Only a supervisor who has the power to make decisions about the target's employment can engage in *quid pro quo* harassment. This is the form of sexual harassment with which most people are familiar and that most people agree is sexual harassment.

The second type of sexual harassment, hostile environment harassment, raises more questions. Hostile environment harassment happens when the actor's unwelcome sexual behavior has one of two kinds of impact. It either interferes with the target's work performance or creates a hostile, offensive, or threatening work environment. The behavior alters the employee's experience of the workplace, causing the work environment to be a sexually charged, intimidating, or offensive place to be. The actor can be a supervisor or a coworker who makes persistent offensive comments or repeatedly has unnecessary physical contact of a sexual nature with the target.

Hostile environment harassment usually requires sexual behavior that is not only unwanted, but is also repeated relatively frequently over a period of time. In general, one event, such as one dirty joke or one kiss on the cheek, will not alter the experience of the work environment and will not be called sexual harassment. Of course, being sexually attacked in the supply closet would certainly alter the target's experience of the workplace, as would one incident of being forcibly fondled by several coworkers at an office party. Daily unwelcome comments from coworkers about one's body parts and what the coworkers would like to do to them would also shift one's experience of the work environment to a sexually charged or hostile environment. Hostile environment harassment also includes a supervisor's unwanted sexual behavior plus a threat to withhold some tangible benefit, where the supervisor never carries out the threat, even if it happens only once.

In 1982, when I was the legal counsel for Hunter College of the City University of New York, I drafted Hunter College's first sexual harassment policy. In several large meetings, designed to orient everyone in the college to the new rules, I explained that certain behavior was now prohibited and that the college would take steps to enforce them.

A few days after Donna Shalala, who was then Hunter's president, issued the new policy, a woman employee came to my office and told me that the men she worked with touched her, pinched her, and spoke to her in vulgar language nearly every day. She said she had heard that President Shalala said what they were doing is wrong and would stop them from bothering her. I asked her who her supervisor was, who had touched her, and exactly what the men had said to her. Then, I asked her how long this behavior had been going on. She answered, "For about nine or 10 years." I was saddened, but moved by the courage it took for this womant to come forward. I gave her a copy of the college's sexual harassment policy and told her that, after we investigated and verified her story, I would make sure the coworkers left her alone.

I walked immediately to the office of the vice president who was responsible for the woman's unit and repeated her story. He responded that the woman must have teased the men or at least have led them on. Then he said, "This kind of thing goes on a lot. That's what life is like down there in that office. Anyway, it's just harmless messing around and there isn't much I can do about it."

I told him that this employee was very upset and that it was unlikely that she had led on the entire staff in her unit for 10 years. In any event, as the employer, we were legally required to investigate her story. If her story was true, the college was in violation of federal and state law unless we took immediate steps to correct the situation.

Following an investigation, we determined that the woman's story was accurate. With President Shalala's support as the president of the college, the vice president instructed the supervisor and the employees in the unit the behavior was to stop immediately. Those involved were disciplined. I checked in with the woman a few weeks later, and she told me the behavior had stopped.

This long-time employee had experienced 10 years of hostile environment harassment. She had suffered no tangible loss. She still had her job and had received appropriate raises, leave time, and other benefits. Nonetheless, she had experienced unwelcome sexual behavior that was so pervasive and ongoing that she experienced the work environment as intimidating, hostile, and offensive.

The question I hear most often about the "hostile environment" is, "Because the same behavior can be offensive to one person and not offensive to another person, how can you know what is acceptable?" The list of actions that would be so severe that one incident would constitute harassment is pretty short. It includes physical assaults, threats of physical harm, and profound humiliation in the presence of other employees. A complete list is impossible to make, because the definition includes the target's perception of whether the behavior is unwelcome or unwanted and the effect of the actor's behavior on the target. A compliment might delight one person and offend another.

The trouble with the definition is that it begins with two words that are very difficult to define, "unwelcome" and "sexual." The legal definition was meant to be used by courts, lawyers, and investigators. The legal definition leaves individuals to struggle to determine what is and is not unwelcome sexual behavior.

When a judge or jury decides whether particular behavior was unwelcome, it has the benefit of having heard the testimony of witnesses, having received physical evidence, and having listened to the presentations of lawyers for both parties. How does an individual employee who wants to approach another know whether particular behavior will be unwelcome?

There are signs that give a good indication whether behavior is unwelcome. The signs of unwelcomeness include statements the target made to the actor or to someone else expressing displeasure. A target who leaves the encounter crying, calls in sick the next day, quits her job, or goes out of her way to avoid the actor may be signaling that the behavior was unwelcome. If the target did not respond to the behavior or responded in a vague or equivocal manner, courts have to look elsewhere to determine whether the behavior was unwelcome.

The next element is whether the behavior interfered with the target's work performance or had the purpose or effect of creating a hostile, offensive, or intimidating work environment. Again, courts look to the target's reaction. Some courts also ask how the behavior would affect the "reasonable woman." Of course, the reasonable woman is not a real person, and the actor cannot ask the reasonable woman how she would react. The reasonable woman, similar to the "reasonable person" in other areas of the law, is what lawyers call a legal fiction, a make-believe person to whom we can pretend to ask the question and then pretend we know how she would respond.

This still leaves the actor with the question: How can I know whether my behavior will be welcome or unwelcome?

If the target expresses or signals displeasure, and you stop the behavior, you have successfully avoided committing sexual harassment. The rules anticipate the possibility of offending someone unwittingly and give the opportunity to stop the behavior.

You can ask in advance. Most workplace cultures do not encourage this kind of open communication, and most of us are not used to engaging in straightforward conversation about personal boundaries. Few of us are skilled in expressing our displeasure at unwanted behavior, sexual or otherwise, and recognizing and respecting what others say. Yet, open, straightforward communication about personal boundaries and respect for others' sensibilities is precisely what is called for if we are to overcome the challenges of the modern workplace.

Following the word "unwelcome," the next word in the definition, "sexual," is also problematic. What is sexual behavior? Is an invitation to lunch sexual behavior? Is an invitation to dinner sexual behavior? What about a compliment on an outfit or a hairdo? The only possible answer is sometimes yes and sometimes no.

Knowing what is and is not sexual harassment begins with a list of generally unacceptable sexual behavior. Any action must be evaluated as to whether the particular target welcomes it and the impact on that target. Once the target expresses displeasure with the behavior, it is up to the actor to stop.

A wide range of behaviors, ranging from the mild to the severe, can be sexual harassment. The test is how severe, frequent, and persistent the behavior is. Physical threats, physical assaults, and physical touches on the breasts, buttocks, legs, and mouth are generally considered to be at the severe end of the spectrum. At the mild end of the spectrum are verbal behavior and visual displays, including unwelcome invitations, proposals, sexual jokes, vulgar comments, excessive and sexually suggestive compliments, sexual e-mails, sexual notes and cartoons, as well as hugs and pats. Verbal behavior and visual displays, even when accompanied by physical behavior, such as gestures and glares, are generally considered to be less severe. Any of these behaviors or any combination of them can create a hostile environment if they are repeated. Whether the behavior is severe or mild, if it is persistent or pervasive, it can create a hostile environment.

The prohibition against sexual harassment was never meant to outlaw flirtatious and playful behavior among employees. Welcome behavior is not sexual harassment. Even unwelcome behavior is not sexual harassment, if it does not result in the target experiencing a tangible loss, interference with the ability to perform his or her job, or a seriously intimidating, hostile, and offensive work environment. Sex-related behavior that is commonplace and expected in the context of one work environment can be offensive, even abusive, in another work environment. A single offensive remark or gesture is not sexual harassment on its own, but if it is repeated, it is sexual harassment when viewed as the beginning of a campaign of intimidation. All the incidents together are the sexual harassment.

Sexual harassment in schools, colleges, and universities that receive federal funds is governed by another section of the Civil Rights Act of 1964, known as Title IX. Sexual harassment in educational institutions is discussed in Chapter 14.

Who is covered?

The federal law covers employers with 16 or more employees, employment agencies, and labor unions. It also covers the employer's agents, suppliers, and consultants. State and local laws vary as to the number of employees an employer must have to be covered. For example, the New York Human Rights Law covers employers with four or more employees.

Can a man be sexually harassed?

Yes. Anyone who works for someone else or attends school can be harassed. A man can be sexually harassed by a woman or by another man. A woman can be harassed by a man or by another woman.

The target can be male, female, black, white, gay, straight, blue collar, white collar, pink collar, supervisor, coworker, or executive. Likewise, the actor can be male, female, black, white, gay, straight, blue collar, white collar, pink collar, supervisor, coworker, or executive. Sexual harassment always goes down the ladder of the organization or across the ladder on the same level. It never goes up the hierarchical ladder. If a subordinate engages in unwanted sexual behavior toward someone in a superior position in the organization, the superior has the power and authority to stop the behavior or to discipline the subordinate.

Some people find it difficult to believe that men can be sexually harassed. It is assumed that men are always interested in sex and would welcome any sexual attention from a woman. This is not true. A woman in a position of power can exploit a male subordinate as effectively as a male boss can exploit a female subordinate. As women have moved into supervisory and management positions, their opportunities to harass men have expanded. There are fewer examples of female-on-male harassment, not only because it does not occur as often, but also because men are even less likely to talk about it than are women. The dynamics may be somewhat different, but the impact is the same.

Hollywood capitalized on this lesser exemplified situation in the 1994 movie *Disclosure*, in which Demi Moore's character seduces her subordinate, played by Michael Douglas. When he interrupts their first intimate encounter, saying he can't go through with it, she retaliates by accusing him of sexually harassing her and begins a campaign to make him lose a promotion and his job.

Man-on-man harassment typically calls up the image of a homosexual acting on his sexual desires for the other homosexual or heterosexual man. According to Catherine MacKinnon in her book, *Sexual Harassment of Working Women*: "Sexual coercion from a gay male superior presents one of the few instances in which an uninterested male employee has a chance of facing a situation similar to that which many women employees commonly face every day—except that he has a better chance than do women of ruining his employer's career if he exposes it." That is one possibility, but it is not the only circumstance in which a man can harass another man.

Take the case of Joseph Oncale, a 21-year-old man who was employed as a roustabout on an oil platform in the Gulf of Mexico off the coast of southern Louisiana. Three of Oncale's fellow workers, including the supervisor, regularly subjected him to humiliating sexual behavior, grabbing him and rubbing their genitals against him. On one occasion, the supervisor and another worker physically assaulted him in a shower stall, forcibly rubbing a bar of soap between his buttocks and threatening to rape him. Oncale's complaints to management produced no results, and he quit, saying it was because of sexual harassment and verbal abuse.

The law is based on the extreme cases, and in this case, it did not matter that Joseph Oncale's fellow workers were not motivated by sexual desire. Their actions were not only sexual, but also deliberate, malicious, frightening, and humiliating. They created an offensive, intimidating, and hostile work environment, making their actions sexual harassment.

Of course, knowing and even understanding the definition of sexual harassment is just the starting point. You have to be able to apply it in practice.

When Supervisors Harass

Michelle Vinson was hired as a teller-trainee at Capitol City Federal Savings and Loan Association in 1974. In the four years she worked there, she was promoted to teller, head teller, and finally to assistant branch manager. The bank fired her in 1978, and she sued her employer for sexual harassment. In the trial, Vinson testified she had engaged in sexual intercourse with her supervisor 50 to 60 times over two and a half years, and she believed that if she refused, she would be fired. She also testified that her supervisor fondled her in front of other employees, followed her into the women's restroom when she went there alone, exposed himself to her, and forcibly raped her on several occasions. Vinson never reported her supervisor's behavior to anyone at the bank. Eventually, she went on sick leave for an indefinite period, and the employer fired her for excessive use of sick leave.

The employer lost the case and was ordered to pay Vinson's lost wages because her supervisor's behavior was unlawful sexual harassment. Michelle Vinson's case was decided in 1986. It was the first time the Supreme Court recognized that sexual harassment was a violation of Title VII of the Civil Rights Act of 1964.

Before 1986, a plaintiff in a sexual harassment case had to show that he or she suffered a measurable economic loss. Vinson's case established the principle that the psychological impact of having to endure unwelcome sexual behavior could constitute hostile environment sexual harassment. A tangible loss of job benefits is not required. This case also addressed the issues of consent and notice to the employer.

This chapter will describe the rules that determine when an employer is responsible for a supervisor's sexually harassing behavior. It will also list what the employer can do to prevent sexual harassment by supervisors and how employees can respond to a supervisor's unwelcome behavior.

The rules that govern the employer's responsibility when a supervisor creates a hostile environment are different from the rules that govern the employer's responsibility for a hostile environment created by a coworker. This is obviously important for employees who want to avoid liability of any kind. It is also important for employees who may be targets of harassing supervisors. The more stringent rules for supervisors acknowledge the dynamics of the relationship between supervisors and subordinates that may affect how the target responds to the behavior.

First, we will look at the employer's responsibility for the behavior of its supervisors. Supervisors are defined as people who have the authority to make employment decisions directly affecting the employee. Supervisors can sexually harass their subordinates in two ways:

- By withholding tangible job benefits from an employee who rejects their unwelcome sexual advances; and

- By creating a hostile work environment that includes threatening to withhold tangible job benefits if an employee rejects their unwelcome sexual advances.

A hostile work environment is engaging in unwelcome sexual behavior that is sufficiently severe to alter the employee's experience of the work environment. A hostile environment includes a supervisor's threat to withhold tangible job benefits from an employee who rejects unwelcome behavior. Chapter 6 discusses hostile environment harassment in more detail.

Sexual harassment by a supervisor is a misuse of supervisory authority. The employer is responsible for the misuse of that authority. If the supervisor withholds tangible job benefits for an employee who rejected the supervisor's unwelcome behavior, the employer is automatically responsible for sexual harassment by means of the supervisor's action.

If the employee suffered no tangible loss, the employer can avoid liability or being ordered to pay damages by showing that it took care to prevent sexually harassing behavior and to correct any sexually harassing behavior that it knew about. The employer must also prove that the employee failed to take advantage of any preventive or corrective opportunities provided by the employer and to avoid harm otherwise.

This rule makes employers responsible for the actions of their supervising employees and provides a defense where there is no tangible economic loss. This is good news and bad news for employers. The good news is that there are situations in which they will not have to pay damages to employees whom a supervisor has sexually harassed. Companies can defend themselves. The bad news is that, in order to defend themselves, employers must show that they have taken care to prevent or correct sexual harassment in their workplaces. The employer must take specific actions. In most situations, the employer must do the following to take care to prevent any sexual harassment: establish a clear policy against sexual harassment, including an accessible complaint procedure; distribute the policy to every employee; explain to employees how to use the complaint procedure; and act promptly to correct any sexual harassment brought to management's attention.

I list on the following two pages the basic steps employers can take to prevent and correct sexual harassment. Chapter 14 describes not only how to create a work environment that prevents sexual harassment, but also reveals elements of the current workplace culture that promote and encourage sexual harassment, gives employees who are not managers and supervisors opportunities to support the employer in preventing sexual harassment, and offers new opportunities to correct both the sources as well as the symptoms of sexual harassment. In the long run, altering the environment will reduce costs, improve employee morale, and increase employee productivity and creativity.

The first part of the employer's obligation is to take care to prevent sexually harassing behavior and to correct any sexually harassing behavior that is known. Specific actions have to be tailored to be effective in the particular workplace. What works to prevent sexual harassment in a small informal workplace may not work in a large corporation. What works for a family-owned business that has employed the same group of employees for many years may not work in a dot-com company with high employee turnover. There are certain basic steps that all employers should take.

To exercise reasonable care to prevent sexually harassing behavior:

- Adopt an antiharassment policy.
- Create a swift and accessible complaint procedure.
- Advise and train supervisors and managers to avoid sexual behavior toward subordinates.
- Advise and train managers and supervisors to avoid treating men and women differently.
- Distribute the policy and procedure to all employees.
- Train all employees in the policy and procedure.
- Post the policy and procedures in conspicuous places.
- Document that every employee received the policy.
- Adopt a complaint procedure that encourages employees to report sexual harassment.
- Train employees on the standards in the policy and how to use the complaint procedure.
- Train supervisors and managers on their responsibility under the policy.
- Train those authorized to receive complaints in receiving, investigating, and evaluating complaints.
- Monitor the effectiveness of the complaint procedure.
- Make periodic reports to employees about the results of complaints under the procedure.

To exercise reasonable care to correct any sexually harassing behavior that the employer knows about:

- Investigate promptly every complaint received.

- Take prompt action on every verified complaint that is designed to prevent the harassment from happening again and restores whatever the tangible loss the target suffered.

- Develop a way to respond to rumors and informal expressions of concern that are not submitted as formal complaints.

- Develop a way to address complaints about which the target requests confidentiality or requests that nothing be done.

The nature of the supervisory relationship

The nature of the supervisory relationship is coercive. A supervisor can terminate, withhold job offers, force transfers, deny promotions, limit pay raises, block bonuses, decline leave, impose assignments, and withhold training. Supervisors have control over employers by virtue of this authority. The supervisor who demands sexual favors in exchange for job benefits wields authority on behalf of the employer, and the law makes the employer responsible for that supervisor's behavior. Most supervisors do not view themselves as coercers.

Saying no to one's supervisor can have consequences, and many people feel they cannot say no to their supervisors, often because they are not in a position to lose their jobs or to quit if things go badly. Although many people have personal boundaries and standards that allow them to say no to inappropriate requests, when someone with a general inability or reluctance to say no, a lack of personal boundaries, or an unwillingness to pay the consequences is confronted with a supervisor's inappropriate demand, the results can be abuse and exploitation.

The fears are not always unfounded. Supervisors often resent employees who say no or who complain about their behavior. The common supervisory culture is that subordinates must do what they demand or suffer grave consequences.

I have seen otherwise patient, understanding, and professional supervisors express bitter indignation when a subordinate has accused them of any kind of discriminatory behavior, including sexual harassment. I have seen supervisors become especially resentful when an employee complained through the established channels instead of complaining directly to the offending supervisor about his or her behavior. The employer and, therefore, the supervisor, cannot require an employee to report sexually harassing behavior to the supervisor precisely because the supervisor may be the person doing the harassing. Supervisors may not be designated as the person to monitor or investigate complaints about their own behavior or the behavior of anyone in their chain of command.

A female manager once complained to me that her manager kissed her on the cheek, as his way of greeting her, instead of shaking her hand. She said that when he shook hands with the men and then kissed her he undermined her authority. She did not know how he would react and was reluctant to speak to him herself. This was no shy, retiring female, but a tough, self-assured professional.

I spoke to her manager about her concern, and he was surprised she had objected. He said he was old-fashioned and kissed women in the office as a sign of affection and respect. I advised him that he had to treat the males and females similarly, especially because there was a perceived difference in treatment that affected their ability to function effectively. He understood her concern and agreed to stop kissing the women.

Most people understand that they can respectfully disagree with their superiors on business matters, but the superior has the last word. It is sometimes difficult to separate the area of personal boundaries as an area where a supervisor might not have the last word.

Some people have a very highly developed ability to differentiate their supervisor's authority in this arena of personal relations/ personal boundaries from the supervisor's authority in the area of office or business matters.

A good friend told me the following story, which took place in the mid-1950s:

My friend was working in a clerical position in an office. Her supervisor was a powerful high-ranking professional in the organization, known in the community as a "ladies man." One day, she was standing at the file cabinet, leaning forward to read the labels on the folders into which she was filing papers. Her supervisor walked up behind her, reached his arms around on either side of her body, placed his hands on the file drawer, and leaned his head over her shoulder, pretending to view the files alongside her. He had effectively boxed her in with his body, an obviously sexual maneuver.

My friend turned her body around so that she faced him, looked him right in the eye, pushed his arm away and walked off. He respected her signal that his behavior was unwelcome and never attempted that or any other sexual behavior with her again. She told me, however, that she knew of other women who had worked for this man before and who had succumbed to his intimidating tactics.

How to recognize and deal with a predatory boss

Most supervisors do not sexually harass their subordinates, but even the most respectful and sensitive supervisor may engage in unwanted sexual behavior. With supervisors, as with coworkers, more often than not the quickest, cheapest, and most effective way to stop unwanted behavior is to speak up and make a request.

Predatory supervisors are the exceptions. A predatory supervisor is one who withholds or threatens to withhold job benefits when a subordinate rejects or expresses concern about his or her unwelcome sexual behavior. A predatory supervisor is also one who ignores, refuses, or ridicules a request to stop the unwelcome behavior. My friend's supervisor was not predatory toward her because he stopped the behavior.

The best way to deal with predatory supervisors is to report them. Unless you plan to lock your predatory supervisor in a closet (as Dolly Parton's, Lily Tomlin's, and Jane Fonda's characters did in the movie *9 to 5*) and you are prepared to go to jail, you need the support of someone with more power than you have on your own.

Never try to negotiate or make a request of a supervisor who withholds or threatens to withhold job benefits in exchange for sexual favors, ignores your expression of concern, or ridicules you.

Your reluctance to tell your supervisor that you don't appreciate his or her behavior toward you is understandable. Nonetheless, unless your supervisor is a predator, you should communicate your concern to your supervisor about his or her unwelcome behavior. Understand that some supervisors, but not all, will respond with understanding and generosity.

Express your concern about the behavior, not about the supervisor's motives or character. If the behavior continues, report him or her to the person designated to receive complaints.

If you are concerned that the supervisor may retaliate against you, communicate your concern. Retaliation, a negative employment decision based on the fact that you objected to or reported the behavior, is a separate offense. Report any retaliation.

Employers and their legal advisors have been understandably concerned about being held liable for behavior about which they have no knowledge and which they did not encourage or condone. This is precisely the situation in which the City of Boca Raton found itself. The officials in city hall had issued an antiharassment policy and procedure, but they failed to tell the Marine Unit, which employed its lifeguards, about the policy.

Beth Ann Faragher v. City of Boca Raton

Beth Ann Faragher worked as a lifeguard with the City of Boca Raton in its Marine Unit between 1985 and 1990. She resigned in 1990 and sued the city, claiming that during the five years when she worked for the Marine Unit, her supervisors made lewd remarks, spoke of women in offensive terms, and subjected her and other female lifeguards to uninvited and offensive touching. One supervisor had touched a female lifeguard, put his arm around her with his hand on her buttocks, made crude references to women, and once commented negatively on Faragher's shape. She also proved this supervisor once made physical contact with another female lifeguard, simulating a sex act. During an interview with a woman he hired as a lifeguard, he said that the female lifeguards had sex with the male lifeguards and asked whether she would do the same. He once said that he would never promote a woman to the rank of lieutenant.

Faragher also proved that a second supervisor engaged in similar behavior. He once commented on having sexual relations with her, and once he said, "Date me or clean toilets for a year." On another occasion he imitated an act of oral sex. Before Faragher resigned, she spoke to a third supervisor about this behavior, who responded, "The city just does not care." She did not consider these conversations to be formal complaints and she never complained to higher management.

The City of Boca Raton was found liable to Faragher for the hostile environment created by the two supervisors. Although the city had established an antiharassment policy, it did not distribute the policy to its employees in the Marine Unit. They had not seen the policy and did not know that the City of Boca Raton prohibited sexual harassment.

Beth Ann Faragher's case led to employers being automatically liable for a hostile environment created by a supervisor with immediate authority over the harassed employee, unless the employer can demonstrate that it exercised reasonable care to prevent and correct harassing behavior and the employee unreasonably failed to take advantage of any preventive or corrective opportunities provided by the employer.

Relationships with subordinates are a bad idea

Supervisors should expect to be accused of discriminating against subordinates, including being accused of sexual harassment. It goes with the territory. In the course of your career, you are bound to do something that offends someone, and someone is bound to complain about you. You should avoid engaging in unwelcome sexual behavior, but if you expect never to be the subject of a sexual harassment complaint about your behavior, you will be disappointed, possibly resentful ("How dare she accuse me?") when it comes. Your disappointment, resentfulness, and indignation may cause you to respond inappropriately.

> **Avoid engaging in unwanted sexual behavior toward your subordinates.**

There is no need to avoid complimenting your employees or engaging in levity with the employees you supervise. Title VII, the federal law prohibiting sex discrimination in employment, was never meant to remove all sexually different treatment from the workplace. It was meant to remove discriminatory barriers to employment.

In any event, do not make overt sexual advances toward your subordinates, as they may not feel free to object to your behavior if it is unwelcome. You may assume that behavior is welcome when it is not.

We hear and see what we want to hear and see. We filter other people's words and actions through our own beliefs and perceptions. If you are attracted to a subordinate, you may perceive his or her behavior in the light most favorable to you. If you are looking for signs that a subordinate welcomes your advances, that is what you will see. It is a natural human tendency, and you cannot trust yourself to evaluate his or her behavior toward you objectively.

> **Resist subordinate-initiated sexual behavior.**

Again, we hear and see what we want to hear and see. We filter other people's words and actions through our own beliefs and perceptions. If you believe a subordinate is making advances toward you, you will perceive his or her behavior in the light most favorable to you. If you are looking for signs that a subordinate is interested in you, that is what you will see. It is a natural human tendency, and you should not trust yourself to evaluate his or her behavior toward you objectively.

> **Don't engage in sexual relationships with your subordinates.**

Office romances can be treacherous to navigate. It may be tempting to indulge an attraction or respond to a flirtation. We all think we can handle these things, but if the relationship ends badly, you may find yourself working with a bitter colleague, or, worse, you may be the bitter partner. You may even be exposing yourself to an accusation of sexual harassment, as the person could claim that you demanded the relationship. This sounds extreme and unlikely, but it does happen.

One approach is to seek a transfer and engage in the relationship when you are no longer the other person's direct supervisor. You could even remove yourself from employment decisions about the other person, while you continue to supervise for other purposes.

> **Encourage your subordinates to tell you if you do something offensive or inappropriate.**

If you encourage your employees to be in communication, you will discover the limits of and create opportunities to respect their personal boundaries. With the support of your upper management, you can have periodic conversations with your employees as a group about what kind of behavior is welcome and unwelcome. This will demonstrate that you have a commitment to the sexual harassment policy and are interested in avoiding a hostile environment and creating a high quality environment.

If an employee approaches you with a concern about your behavior, thank the employee for bringing the matter to your attention, agree not to engage in the offensive behavior, and seek out immediate advice on how to resolve the situation from your manager, human resources department, or Equal Employment Opportunity officer.

You could try treating men and women similarly. If you compliment women on their new hairdos, compliment men on their new haircuts. If you compliment women on their new outfit, compliment the men on their new suits. If you comment that a female employee is looking buff as the result of her recent commitment to working out, comment on how well the guys are doing, too. This may seem awkward and unnatural at first. We are altering behavior after all. If this seems unreasonable to you, then you have a gender agenda, and you should review the self-assessment tool in Chapter 5.

From time to time, an employee may approach a trusted person in the organization, often another supervisor than his or her own, someone who is not the person designated to receive complaints. I discuss more expansively in Chapter 9 how to respond when an employee complains. The critical things to do if an employee brings a concern to you about another supervisor's behavior are to listen, affirm the employer's antiharassment policy, and direct the employee to the person designated to receive complaints under the employer's complaint procedure. The critical things not to do are to be dismissive, patronize the employee, withhold or cover up the employee's complaint, or discourage the employee from making a formal complaint by taking the complaint to the designated person.

The bottom line for supervisor sexual harassment:

- Employers are automatically liable for the sexually harassing behavior of supervisors where a tangible employment decision was made.

- Employers are automatically liable for the hostile environment created by a supervisor, unless the employer took reasonable care to prevent and correct promptly any sexually harassing behavior and the employee unreasonably failed to take advantage of preventive or corrective opportunities or to avoid harm.

- The target should communicate his or her concerns to a supervisor or the person designated to receive complaints.

- The target should report any supervisor who withholds or threaten to withhold job benefits or ignores an expression of concern.

- Supervisors should avoid sexual behavior toward and sexual relationships with their subordinates.

- Supervisors should respond positively to subordinates who object to their unwanted behavior.

- Supervisors should encourage subordinates to communicate concerns.

- Supervisors should affirm the employer's sexual harassment policy.

- Supervisors who learn of a sexual harassment complaint about another supervisor should direct the employee to the person designated to receive complaints.

- Employers should issue a sexual harassment policy, create a procedure for prompt corrective action, and encourage employees to use the procedure.

- Employers should make sure all employees know about and understand the policy and procedure.

5

Hostile Environment Harassment

Catherine MacKinnon, a noted expert in sexual harassment whose work was critical in the development of this area of the law, says in her book, *Sexual Harassment of Working Women*, "The sexual harassment may occur as a single encounter or as a series of incidents at work."

If unwanted sexual attention continues and creates a situation at the workplace where the employee's experience of his or her work environment is one of intimidation, hostility, or offense, or if job performance is impaired because of having to tolerate or because of the attention, it is a situation that falls within the definition of hostile environment harassment.

In sexual harassment workshops, I give the participants a copy of the definition of sexual harassment and read it aloud line by line. During one workshop for government employees, I asked: "How many times can an employee ask another employee for a dinner date before he crosses the line into sexual harassment?" A female manager responded, "Three." Someone else said, "Four." A woman with blond hair in the front row said, "He can ask twice. If she says no the first time, the second time is sexual harassment."

I asked, "How do you decide what number is the right number of times?"

A man, sitting to my right, near the back said, "You know how women are. You can't tell if she really doesn't want to go out with you. She might be going out with someone else, but it's not going so well. She might want to go out with you, but she says no because of the other guy. You have to ask her again."

I asked him to tell me more about the woman who says no, but really wants to say yes. He replied, "It happens all the time. She's not sure, or she thinks it's not right to say yes. Sometimes they don't know what they're doing." Some of the women in the room began to talk among themselves, disagreeing vehemently with what he said. Some laughed. Others looked at the man angrily.

"How can you tell," I asked him, "whether this woman means no, or doesn't know what she means?"

"You have to keep asking her," he said. "Maybe she doesn't know you well enough to go out with you. Maybe she likes you, but she thinks she shouldn't."

"But how do you find out?"

"You keep asking."

A woman shouted at him, "That's stupid! What a joke! How can you say something like that?"

I told the group, "It is important for you to know what the men you are working with think and how they hear what you say. His opinion is real, and I promise you that if this is what he's thinking, other men think the same thing. Let's talk about what you want him to do rather than to keep asking you out."

"He could just take no for an answer."

I asked the man, "What about taking no for an answer? Could you do that?"

"I'd want to find out whether she would go out with me."

"What makes you think she might say yes, even though she said no."

"I guess it's the way she says it. It's the nature of men to pursue women," he explained, "And no amount of education is going to change that."

The pursuit of female company or sexual satisfaction is one thing, but using one's authority as a supervisor or taking advantage of the woman's inability to escape the attention without leaving her job is another thing altogether.

● ● ●

This exchange demonstrates the difficulty of establishing the line that separates sexual harassment from acceptable social interaction. Some of us claim the right to pursue sexual conquest on and off the job, but we want to know just how far we can go and still claim we made an innocent social invitation or engaged in harmless banter.

A woman or a man on the job is a captive audience. The debate arises between people who view every encounter between men and women as a potential opportunity to pursue sexual interest and people who view the workplace as the place where employees do the work they were hired to do.

If we start from the premise that women on the job are there for making matches with men, then the line drawing does become difficult. (It is true that some are, but most are not.) I prefer to start from the premise that people go to work to do their jobs. The law says that they are entitled to do this without having to confront persistent, unwanted sexual attention.

This brings us to the matter of what is unwelcome. An advance is unwelcome when the other person does not welcome the advance. The dictionary (*Concise Oxford Dictionary*, 1976) defines welcome as a kind or glad recognition of a person; ungrudgingly permitting a person to do something; giving someone the right to do something. This definition means that an advance is welcome if the target gives a clear, glad acceptance of the attention.

People in my workshops often ask me, "How can I tell that someone doesn't welcome the attention?" There are certain kinds of attention that we can presume are not welcome: An assault or a lewd reference to the person's body, as in "I'd love to bury my head in those breasts of yours," said to a person with whom the actor does not already have an intimate relationship.

But what if a comment or invitation could be either welcome or unwelcome?

If the target says no or tells the actor to stop making intimate references or touching, the attention is unwelcome.

The men in my workshops have difficulty interpreting two kinds of responses. The first difficult-to-interpret response is when the woman says no, but gives an excuse ("I'm busy that day," "I have a boyfriend," "I don't think so," "I don't think that's such a good idea," "I don't date married men," "My mother is in town," "I need to make this an early night," "I don't usually eat lunch.").

The other difficult-to-interpret response is the positive response from a target who really does not welcome the attention. This situation occurs frequently when the actor is the target's supervisor or other person in the organization whom the target feels she cannot refuse without risking trouble.

I urge men and women who are interested in someone at work to follow these guidelines:

1. Respect the other person's right to do his or her job without having to deal with your social overtures, and

2. Wait for a clear, enthusiastic, positive response. If you do not get one, leave the other person alone.

The fact is that some men actually believe that women do not know what they want or that they will not say what they want.

If the target says no, then the actor must accept the answer. Working together requires that each person accept and respect every other person's wishes. You may believe that a relationship with you would be good for this woman. You may even want to rescue her from a bad or waning relationship with someone else. But it is not the actor's job to decide what the target wants or needs.

Unfortunately, some of us do not say no when we mean no. It is not only women who fail to say clearly what they mean. Many of us, as children, learned to suppress our desires. We also learned that it is rude to say no when others invite us to play or ask us to share. Of course, some children grow up to be more assertive, or more compliant, than others.

But, in general, compliant, cooperative behavior carries over into adulthood.

Cooperative behavior is not bad. Cooperative and compliant behavior are necessary in a civilized society. It will not work to have everyone doing exactly what he or she wants, when he wants and how she wants all the time. However, cooperation and compliant behavior do not have to translate into timidity.

On the other hand, most people do not like to be told no. When you combine the reluctance to say no and the resistance to hearing no, you have a situation that is ripe for misunderstanding.

Every exchange is an opportunity to become aware of another person's boundaries. As actors, we want to know what the rules are. Then we can do what we feel like doing and, so long as we are inside the rules, can avoid making mistakes. We can also justify or explain what we have done because we "followed the rules."

As targets, we want to know what the rules are, so we can assess the behavior of others as okay or not okay.

Knowing the rules allows us to avoid ever really being in communication. It is easier to decide what to do based on what we already know than it is to communicate with another person.

The rules governing sexual harassment do not give the kind of certainty we want. The rules only offer large categories of behavior that might or might not be sexual harassment, depending on the circumstances. Discovering or revealing what is appropriate behavior is an exercise in communication and paying attention. The challenge is to respect our coworkers' boundaries.

The employer's liability for sexual harassment by a coworker

The rules are significantly different when the person who engages in the sexually harassing behavior action is a coworker with no supervisory responsibility. Because an employee's coworker has no authority to take tangible employment action, sexual harassment by a coworker cannot result in a tangible job loss. An employer will be liable for sexual harassment by a coworker if the employer knew or should have known of the harassing behavior or if the employer failed to take prompt corrective action. If the employer did not know of the harassment or if the behavior was not so severe or pervasive that the employer should have known about it, the employer cannot be held liable for a coworker's sexually harassing behavior.

Once it is established that the employer had knowledge or should have had knowledge of the harassment, the employer will be liable if it failed to take prompt correction action. Courts have dismissed claims of plaintiffs where the report to the supervisor was not detailed enough to establish knowledge; where the employee did not report the harassment to the company at all; and where the complaint was made to a supervisor, but not to upper management. Two employees were awarded more than $200,000 each because their employers didn't act when they complained about sexual harassment and did not have a sexual harassment policy or complaint procedure.

Most of us do not pay attention to what's happening around us; we are not interested in other peoples' experiences;

and we do not listen to what other people say. We pay attention to what we are concerned about. We are interested in our own concerns and we hear what we want to hear. Contrary to the opinion of many women, this is not a male condition; it is a human condition. It is also a huge disadvantage in navigating the gray area of sexual harassment.

Self-Assessment Tool

I've developed a three-level tool for assessing your own behavior before you do or say anything that may be in the gray area. To use this tool, ask yourself the questions at each level. There are three levels on which you may be interacting:

1. Innocent interaction
2. Gender-specific agenda
3. Hostile agenda

Innocent interaction

Ask yourself whether your behavior is sexual, teasing, or patronizing in nature, such that it could possibly be offensive. If the answer is yes, don't do it. An innocent greeting has no agenda and is not seeking to provoke a response. Ask yourself, "Would I say or do the same thing if the target were the other gender?" In other words, if this woman were a man, would I say the same thing? Or if this man were a woman, would I say the same thing? If the answer is yes, then it's an innocent interaction, and you can proceed, assured that there is no realistic potential of sexual harassment. If your answer is no, then you have a gender agenda, and you must assess your agenda by considering other factors.

Gender-specific agenda

Gender-specific comments and actions run the risk of being sexually harassing. Gender-specific comments include flirtatious remarks; comments about specific body parts; questions about the other person's social life; invitations to lunch, dinner, drinks, or dates; unsolicited advice on dress, makeup, looking sexy, and getting along with you or others. Remarks in this category can be sexually harassing if they are not welcomed by the person to whom you are speaking.

Ask yourself: Is this comment welcomed? A sure indication the behavior was unwelcome is if the person says, "I don't like what you just said (or did)." If someone says that, stop what you are doing, apologize, and don't do it again.

What if the target says nothing, laughs nervously, changes the subject, cuts the conversation short, or pulls away from you? These are all signs that your behavior may be unwelcome. Unfortunately, human beings tend to mask their true feelings. We are taught to be polite, whatever the circumstances. Women, in particular, will sometimes avoid hurting another person's feelings, even when they are faced with offensive or demeaning behavior.

What can you do if the target doesn't say that your behavior is unwelcome? There are three options. The first is to abandon all gender-specific conversation. This is unrealistic for most people. Gender is an ever-present fact of life. Even if we could ignore gender, we would rob ourselves of a rich and necessary aspect of relating to other human beings.

The second option is to "just ask." Simply say to the target, "You know, this sexual harassment stuff has me very confused and reluctant to say anything friendly or compli-mentary at work. Would it bother you if I complimented you on your dress?" If the target says that it is not a problem, then you are on safe territory. The comment would be wel-come, and so it would not be sexually harassing behavior.

There are two exceptions to the "just ask" option. The first exception is women who are not free to say no to you. This will include your subordinates; that is, women to whom you are superior in the organization. You should expect such women to say "no problem," even if they find your remarks are completely inappropriate. They will not want to offend you. Another exception is minors and very young women (aged 18 to 25). I list minors as an exception because, in general, they cannot be held responsible for your behavior, and they can't be expected to consider that what they say could impact your behavior. Very young women are an exception because often they have not yet developed the self-esteem that would allow them to speak up for themselves in an unpleasant situa-tion, especially an unpleasant work situation.

The third option is to learn what is generally acceptable and not acceptable in your workplace and then use the three-pronged system to assess your behavior for behavior that isn't on the list. Here is a list:

- Commenting on a person's body.
- Making graphic sexual comments.
- Asking someone about his or her sex life, sexual practices, or sexual preferences.
- Talking about your own sex life, sexual practices, or sexual preferences.

- Inviting a person for a social event (lunch, dinner, movies, drinks, a walk, and so on) when he or she has previously turned you down.

- Touching someone without his or her permission

- Speaking about your personal feelings toward another person without explicit permission to do so.

This is not an exhaustive list. That is, other kind of behavior could be sexual harassment. You can assume that these behaviors are unacceptable.

Hostile agenda

If your actions are gender-specific, you could have a hostile agenda. You have a hostile agenda if you aren't willing to ask how the other person feels about your behavior, if you aren't interested in how the other person feels about your behavior, if you give the other person no opportunity to say no to your behavior, or if you continue any behavior after being asked to stop. Actions inside a hostile agenda are sexual harassment if they are severe or if they are repeated. Examples include: Demanding that employees wear skimpy, sexual clothing; telling clients or implying that they can have sex with employees; giving an employee lingerie, hygiene items, or a sex toy as a gift; showing a pornographic movie in a staff meeting; propositions; telling gross sexual jokes, teasing, hooting, making sexual remarks of any kind; whistling at an employee; displaying or delivering pornographic pictures or cartoons; sexual teasing, such as simulating masturbation or sexual intercourse; and imitating the person in a mocking sexual manner.

A hostile agenda also includes touching if it is severe behavior. Severe actions include sexual assault, rape, forced or unsolicited kissing, touching a person's private body parts (breasts, buttocks, genitals, thighs), or touching a person repeatedly or after the other person has objected.

Now, you've read through the categories and lists, and you can't find your situation. First of all, congratulations on getting this far. Second, trust me: your situation is there. If you are a supervisor, read Chapter 4. There is probably someone at your workplace whom you really like. You want to ask him or her out as the prelude to a possible romance. It doesn't look like an innocent interaction because you answered no to the question, "Would you say or do the same thing if the person's gender were different?" You don't think it looks like a hostile agenda because you really like this person and don't feel hostile toward her. Let's review the elements of the hostile agenda. If you feel no need to find out whether the other person welcomes your behavior, and you persist in the behavior anyway, you have a hostile agenda, and you are engaging in sexual harassment. It does not matter whether you feel as though you are not being hostile.

6

The High Cost of Sexual Harassment Lawsuits

Employers pay millions of dollars each year in settlement costs and jury awards to resolve employees' sexual harassment complaints. From 1992 to 2002, the amount employers paid to settle employees' sexual harassment lawsuits rose from about $10 million to about $50 million annually. In 2003, the average jury award in a sexual harassment case was $450,000. Recent judgments against corporate employers for sexual harassment include some of the country's largest and best-known companies.

• • •

In a recent settlement with the EEOC, Nine West, the major retailer of women's shoes and apparel, and its parent company, the Jones Apparel Group, agreed to pay $600,000 to several current and former female employees who claimed they were subjected to sexual harassment, national origin harassment, and retaliation. The EEOC's lawsuit alleged that two high-level managers at Nine West's White Plains, New York, Headquarters groped the women, solicited them for sex, made sexually explicit comments, and taunted some of them with insults about their Hispanic origin. Despite the women's complains to the company, the

EEOC charged, it did nothing to stop or prevent the harassing behavior. The settlement calls for monetary damages to be paid to the women, training for all employees and managers in employment discrimination law, and periodic reports to the EEOC about new discrimination complaints.

• • •

A UPS loader in Iowa won $80.75 million from UPS when a jury decided she was subjected to sexual harassment. In a 2006 case against UPS, a San Francisco jury awarded $63,000 to an openly lesbian worker for sexual harassment during five years. Her supervisor and fellow workers had made disparaging comments about her appearance as not feminine enough and denied her work and safety equipment that was available to male employees.

• • •

An employee won $1 million in lost wages and $50 million in punitive damages in a lawsuit against corporate giant Wal-Mart for sexual harassment. A court later reduced the plaintiff's punitive damages to $5 million because it thought that amount was large enough to punish Wal-Mart and to convince it and other employers that it is important to prevent sexual harassment.

• • •

A jury in Tennessee awarded a male plaintiff $475,000 in compensatory damages and $1.6 million in punitive damages after finding that he was sexually harassed by his homosexual supervisor at the Walden Book Company.

• • •

Susan Barth, the first female police officer in Moneka, Illinois, sued the village of Moneka and two police sergeants for sexual harassment and was awarded nearly $2 million in damages, lost wages, and punitive damages after a three-week trial. Ms. Barth testified at the trial that other officers regularly watched *The Howard Stern Show* (a television show known for its sexual content and offensive language) as they gathered for the roll call before the night shift. During the show, the men regularly made vulgar comments and sometimes compared Barth's body parts to those of the scantily clad female guests on the show, some of whom were strippers and porn stars. She complained to the police department and claimed she quit her job after four years because male officers who were upset by her complaints refused to back her up on police calls.

• • •

In 2006, a jury in Miami awarded $1.34 million to four female employees of Associated Security Enforcement Systems after one of the owners groped one employee's breasts, requested sex in exchange for money, invited the employees for overnight stays, and asked for oral sex. One of the company's employees testified that the owner ordered her to falsify personnel records of one of the plaintiffs in an attempt to cover up his actions. The verdict included $300,000 in punitive damages for each of the four employees.

• • •

A San Diego jury awarded $6.5 million in a sexual harassment case against UltraStar Cinemas, a movie-theater chain. Two theater managers put a knife blade to the throats of two teenaged employees, restrained them, and touched them inappropriately.

• • •

Most of these employers had a policy in place that prohibited sexual harassment, but having a policy is not enough. Employers risk lawsuits and costly verdicts when they fail to investigate employees' sexual harassment complaints, when the investigation is inadequate, when the investigator unreasonably concludes the harassment did not happen, or when they fail to take corrective action. Employers are most vulnerable to legal costs when supervisors harass employees or retaliate against employees who complain. Employers who have a policy that works in practice can avoid liability for the actions of coworkers by showing that the employee did not take advantage of the available procedure or corrective options that were offered.

● ● ●

A recent federal jury verdict, handed down in late October 2006, highlights the importance of avoiding retaliating against an employee who complains of sexual harassment. Kimberely Osorio, the first female editor of *Source* magazine, the so-called bible of hip-hop, sued the New York City–based magazine and its two co-owners for subjecting her to sexual harassment and gender discrimination that included sexually graphic material, raunchy language, and threats of physical violence. She claimed the executives watched pornography and called female employees "bitches" on a regular basis. She also claimed that, when she complained to the company's human resources officer about a hostile workplace, owner Raymond Scott fired her in an angry foul-mouthed tirade an audiotape of which was played at the trial. The jury found that the defendants had not discriminated against Osorio, but the jury agreed that the defendants had retaliated against her.

Osorio was awarded a total of $12 million in damages for the retaliation and an additional $3.5 million against Scott for defamation.

• • •

Many cases are settled before they get to trial or during a trial. Unlike a jury award, a settlement does not establish that the claimed harassment actually occurred. Typically, employers do not admit the sexual harassment occurred as part of a settlement agreement. Employers settle lawsuits for different reasons: to avoid losing at trial, to avoid the expense and business interruption of defending the case, to avoid the exposure of damaging or sensitive information as part of a trial, to counteract negative publicity (because the person whose behavior in the issue is no longer associated with the company), or other reasons.

• • •

Pepsi-Cola General Bottlers, Inc. agreed to pay $400,000 in damages, back pay, and attorney's fees in a sexual harassment case brought by a former dispatcher, Renaee N. Weeks. Ms. Weeks claimed that, during her three years of employment, male employees repeatedly made vulgar sexual comments, asked for dates and sex, touched her, and wrote sexual graffiti about her in the men's restroom. After she made numerous complaints to her supervisors, Weeks said she was terminated.

• • •

A former officer of the Maryland Corrections Department, Lashawna Jones, received $250,000 to settle her federal sexual harassment lawsuit. She alleged a fellow officer and a sergeant propositioned her sexually, assaulted her, exposed their genitals to her, touched her sexually, and made repeated vulgar comments. In one incident, she said a fellow corrections officer shoved his head into her crotch and made vulgar comments. Jones said she was warned that female guards who complained about sexual harassment could be killed and the inmates told her she should fear the other guards. A lawyer for the department said the charges were not substantiated in the internal investigation.

• • •

In a landmark sexual harassment settlement with the EEOC, Morgan Stanley, the Wall Street brokerage firm, agreed to pay $54 million to settle a class action suit brought on behalf of 340 female employees. The lawsuit charged the firm had systematically denied female employees equal pay and promotions excluded them from male-only meetings with clients it hosted at strip clubs and golf games, and tolerated male employees groping women and making lewd comments. Twelve million dollars of the money were paid to Allison Scheiffelin, the lead plaintiff, who also charged she was sexually harassed. A total of $52 million was earmarked for distribution among the female employees, while $2 million supported diversity programs and antidiscrimination activities to create equity and career advancement for women in Morgan Stanley.

• • •

Wall Street giants Merrill Lynch and Salomon Smith Barney settled private class action lawsuits in which each firm had paid out more than $100 million each to female employees who charged they were sexually harassed and denied promotions and dqual compensation in favor of male employees.

• • •

Wal-Mart settled two sexual harassment cases with the EEOC, agreeing to pay $315,000 to three of its female associates who claimed a store assistant manager and a store manager touched, fondled, and grabbed them; propositioned them; and made vulgar, unwanted comments.

• • •

In a series of four lawsuits over three years from 2004 to 2006, the EEOC has successfully sought to crack down on sexual harassment of teenaged employees:

• • •

A federal district court in Rochester, New York granted a $585,000 verdict in a lawsuit the EEOC filed against a national basement waterproofing company, Everdry Waterproofing, whose male managers and salesmen had subjected 13 female employees to a hostile work environment. Most of the employees represented in the lawsuit were teenagers still in high school. The EEOC said at trial that virtually every day over a period of four years, male managers hit the young women on their buttocks, grabbed their breasts, and pressured them for sex. A 16-year-old woman was coerced into having her toes sucked by her male manager on the first day of work as coworkers watched. The verdict represents compensation for lost wages, emotional pain and suffering, and punitive damages.

• • •

Two Burger King franchises agreed to pay $400,000 to settle an EEOC lawsuit that claimed seven female employees were subjected to a hostile environment harassment that consisted of groping, sexual comments, and demands for sex on the job. According to the EEOC's claims, several of the employees, six of whom were high school students, complained to their restaurant and district managers, but nothing was done to stop the behavior.

• • •

Carmike Cinemas based in Raleigh, North Carolina, agreed to pay $765,000 to settle a lawsuit filed by the EEOC on behalf of 14 employees, all teenaged boys, whose male supervisor had groped them and made sexual advances toward them.

• • •

An Albuquerque, New Mexico, McDonald's franchise, Pand Enterprises, Inc., settled a sexual harassment and retaliation lawsuit for $90,000. The lawsuit alleged that a male supervisor harassed male teenaged workers by touching them, requesting sex, and making sexual remarks. The lawsuit also alleged that, when one young man objected to the behavior, his work hours were cut in retaliation. In addition to the settlement money, the employer was required to train employees and prevent future discrimination.

• • •

Large and small employers in all industries and sectors can be vulnerable to sexual harassment lawsuits. Simple prevention activities can dramatically reduce the risk of lawsuits and exorbitant costs. Unfortunately, it is not possible to eliminate the risk of being sued, and it costs even to win.

No one really wins a sexual harassment lawsuit. Lawsuits against employers typically take at least three years to conclude, and some have taken longer than 10 years. Even after an employee wins a jury award, the employer often appeals, leading to more expense and waiting. The "winning" employees, especially women in male-dominated arenas, frequently seek employment in another field.

Part II

• • •

Shifting the
Course
of
Events

7

What to Do If You Are Sexually Harassed

If you experience unwelcome sexual behavior at work and believe you have been sexually harassed, taking the following nine steps will allow you to take charge of the situation and, if necessary, support your employer to resolve the situation.

1. Admit you have a problem.

2. Tell the person whose behavior concerns you the specific behavior you object to and what you want him or her to do or stop doing.

3. Tell someone you trust about the problem.

4. Get a copy of your employer's sexual harassment policy and read it.

5. Keep a diary of everything that happens, including names, dates, events, and how you feel.

6. If the behavior does not stop, report the behavior to the person in the company or agency who is responsible for sexual harassment complaints and insist on a response.

7. Cooperate with the investigation.

8. Complain to an external agency if you cannot identify the person responsible for sexual harassment complaints, if the responsible person does not inform you of the results or the investigation, or if you are not satisfied with the results.

9. Consult a lawyer and decide whether to sue your employer.

1. Admit you have a problem.

Often the person who experiences sexual harassment will be confused or embarrassed and wonder what he or she did to cause someone to treat her this way. He or she may even quit the job, thinking that nothing can be done. Admitting there is a problem is the first step in resolving any problem, including one involving sexual harassment. Having a problem does not mean that there is something wrong with you. Acknowledging the problem will help you to focus on the facts, what you need to do, and whether the other person's behavior is unlawful, and less on your feelings. It is natural to feel bad when you are treated badly. Demeaning, insulting, or threatening behavior can drive up already existing feelings of low self-esteem or worthlessness. Intimidating behavior may make you feel powerless to do anything about it. You can feel as though your whole world is collapsing around you, especially if the person whose behavior is the problem is your direct supervisor. Admitting that you have a problem is the only way to get into action and get something done about your situation.

Be prepared to find out that the behavior is not sexual harassment at all. Refer to the discussion in Chapter 3 to help you determine whether the behavior falls within the definition of sexual harassment.

Sexual harassment (unwelcome sexual behavior) and sexual banter (wanted sexual behavior) are two sides of the same coin, the bizarre result of two cultures coming together. One side of the coin is the sexual culture in which the male pursues the female and the female feigns disinterest, while giving the male hints of encouragement. The male's job is to give chase. In a world where women stayed in the home, she could disappear into the protection of her family if the behavior was unwanted, or until she decided the behavior was unwanted. If and when the female submits, it is a victory for the male. When the female has determined that submission will get her what she wants, it is also a victory for the female. The point here is that it is the male's job to give chase until the female submits. It is the female's job to choose. It is the family's job to protect the female from the pursuer. (This is largely what makes domestic abuse, incest, and child molestation so despicable. The family is supposed to protect its females and children. When females and children are abused inside the family, we are all shocked and offended.)

Of course, this culture is a myth for many women. Some women have always had to work and have historically experienced mistreatment at the hands of men in the workplace. Slave women were repeatedly raped by their masters and their masters' sons. Women in certain immigrant groups suffered terrible abuse in sweat shops and factories. Their families, particularly their men, had no power to protect them. On the other side of the coin and in sharp contrast is the culture of the women's movement, sometimes called women's liberation, which, in the last century, freed women from traditional stereotypes of acceptable positions. Women were able to work outside the home and to have a career, instead of being limited to the roles of homemaker and mother. Women's liberation brought along with it the sexual liberation of women. The universal availability of the birth control pill and other forms of birth control also freed women from concerns about pregnancy, one of the major deterrents from sexual activity. Freed from concerns about pregnancy, women simultaneously became available socially, physically, and sexually. With the traditional restraints removed, women were suddenly, and at the same time open for social interaction, physically present in the workplace, and available for sex to a degree that was never before possible.

When the new culture of women's liberation collided with the older culture of pursuit and protection, a new reality began to emerge. The new reality juxtaposes two irreconcilable cultures. What remains is a bizarre cultural phenomenon in which males pursue and females feign disinterest, while giving the male hints of encouragement. With the lifting of the traditional social and sexual constraints on women, the traditional protection of families, brothers, and fathers disappeared. The new culture says that women, as intelligent, talented, and capable beings, can take care of themselves as well as men can. Without the traditional protection of the family, females no longer have a place to which they can retreat. What is missing, however, are new skills that allow men and women to deal with the new reality. Without new skills, females retreat into old behaviors that worked in the older culture, but no longer work inside the new reality.

Unless and until women learn how to address both welcome and unwelcome sexual advances in the moment of the occurrence in a responsible manner, or men learn to recognize and respond to indications that their advances are welcome or unwelcome, women will suffer as victims of male sexual aggression and men will be labeled as sexual predators.

Admitting that you have a problem includes acknowledging that you are a part of this modern cultural mix. Attracting sexual attention is not the problem. The problem occurs when we attract someone from whom we do not want attention. Attracting someone from whom you do not want sexual attention is a problem, because most women do not have the skills to respond. As women, we are culturally predisposed to preserve harmony, or at least civility. Instead of saying no or asking for what we want, we are likely to be polite and charming in an attempt to preserve a positive working relationship. This is the outdated remnant of the pursuit and protect culture of which we all are a part.

In the face of an unwelcome sexual advance, consider that you don't have the skills to do anything else. You may eventually express your displeasure, but as a woman, expressing displeasure, confronting, and saying no are acts of defiance and a last resort. Our training and cultural disposition limit our choices in how to behave. We want to seek protection. Unfortunately, our fathers and brothers are not there to defend us. It is not surprising that many women who believe they have been sexually harassed say and do nothing or leave their jobs to escape the behavior.

The law has been interposed to serve the protective role once provided by families. The law of sexual harassment and employers' sexual harassment policies are an attempt to create a substitute for the protection of family. As a substitute protector, the law has disadvantages. The law is designed to provide a remedy. Sometimes it can serve as a deterrent. The law does not and cannot prevent or stop the unwelcome behavior. The law takes time. While remedies are available, it can take months or years to pursue a lawsuit to completion.

However useful and necessary they are, employers' sexual harassment policies and procedures also have disadvantages. First, the employer's policy and procedure involve a process that takes time. In clear-cut, egregious situations of sexual harassment, employers have been known to act swiftly and decisively to stop the behavior and remedy the situation. However, most situations are neither clear-cut, nor egregious. As such, they require time. Investigation, analysis, and decision. It can take weeks for many employers to act on some situations. Second, employers' policies are designed to limit the employer's liability, which is not the same as being designed to protect employees. For example, employers are now required to provide sexual harassment training, but there is no requirement to demonstrate that the training is effective, has reduced incidents of sexual harassment, or has altered attitudes or behavior in the particular workplace. So long as the employer can demonstrate it has provided training of some kind to every employee, it has met the training requirement. Third, employers may not feel an obligation to act if the behavior hasn't reached the level of sexual harassment. In a situation where the actor hasn't repeated the behavior, the employer doesn't have an obligation to act until there has been sufficient behavior to constitute sexual harassment. This leaves the employee on his or her own until the damage has been done. Finally, employers have the competing motivation to protect their valued employees. Many employers are reluctant to take action against high-level or highly productive employees.

Even with the law and your employer's policy, you have a problem: How to affect another person's behavior in an environment that does not offer protection and where you haven't developed the skills to protect yourself.

> **The first needed skill is to recognize old behaviors that are not effective.**

Women sometimes engage in behaviors that both confuse men and encourage inappropriate sexual behavior. They do not speak up when they welcome sexual behavior. Trained that women must encourage the pursuit, a woman can be passive and aloof when a man in whom she is interested approaches her. Different women behave differently, but the chances are good that a woman will not give a clear, positive response to a welcomed advance. Courting or mating rituals demand vague, nonverbal signals. Women who act too interested ruin the man's need to pursue her. So, the rules of engagement require some encouragement, but not too much.

On the other hand, women can be friendly and accommodating when a man in whom she is not interested approaches her. Again, different women behave differently, but the chances are good that a woman will likewise not give a clear negative response to an unwelcome advance. Women tend to focus on preserving harmony and on nurturing relationships. Women are unlikely to decline an invitation outright or tell a man he is barking up the wrong tree. She is more likely to give an excuse. Common excuses, or lies, are she is busy, has to work through lunch, or has boyfriend, when she isn't busy, doesn't have to work late, and doesn't have a boyfriend. The psychology behind these responses isn't as important as the fact that it confuses men.

Women who operate this way continue to make excuses until the behavior becomes annoying, upsetting, offensive, or intolerable. On reaching this point, she may finally say something. The communication is an explosion of upset.

The first skill is to recognize old behaviors that don't work. One old behavior that doesn't work is pretending not to like what you like and pretending to like what you don't like. When you don't say what you like and what you don't like, it's confusing. A new behavior to learn is to be straight. Say what you like and don't like.

A second behavior that doesn't work is resorting to humor, charm, and cuteness. When you are laughing, people assume you are enjoying yourself. If you say you are not enjoying what is happening, but you laugh when you say it, the laughter may diffuse the situation and make you feel more comfortable. You will not be communicating that you do not like the behavior. It will also not communicate a clear request to stop the specific behavior. I love humor and charm; humor and charm are important aspects of life. Without humor and charm, our workplaces would be unbearably serious and sterile. But there are times when humor and charm don't work.

2. **Tell the person whose offensive, hostile or intimidating behavior concerns you specifically what behavior you object to and what you want him or her to do or stop doing.**

Your most important objectives are to stop the harassing and to get back anything you may have lost. If you suffered any negative employment actions, such as being passed over for a promotion, a pay raise, a transfer, or a training program important to your career advancement, you will want to recover any tangible economic benefit you may have lost. You may also have lost your innocence, your trust in someone with whom you work, and many nights of sleep. Now is not the time for revenge. We'll look later at what the company can and should do to correct the situation. For now, however, you are going to focus on stopping the harassment and recovering anything tangible you have lost.

The first critical step in stopping the harassment is to ask the person to stop the behavior. Do this effectively. Effectively means in a manner that is calculated to get the person to stop. It does not mean calculated to show how angry you are. State calmly and clearly to the person what behavior you want stopped and what you want done. For example, "John, I don't like it when you call me 'slut' and 'bitch'. It's insulting and in front of the staff, it is demeaning. Please call me by my name or not at all." Or, "Michael, this is the second time you've touched me in an inappropriate way. I don't want or need a back rub. Don't touch me again." Don't speak in anger. Don't "make nice," and don't worry about what he'll think. Be concerned about delivering a clear, unmistakable communication and a making a specific request. Many people who engage in offensive or intimidating behavior will stop when they are told clearly the specific actions that are offensive and asked to stop. Some harassers don't get the message the first time, and you may have to repeat your demand. If you would be more comfortable writing a letter, by all means do so. Ask a trusted colleague or friend to read the letter first, and keep a copy. Even if your no doesn't stop the behavior, having said no, you have made the request. You can later establish that you made it clear that you were not interested in the attention.

You must communicate immediately or reasonably quickly after the behavior occurs. No response communicates agreement or acquiescence.

Some targets never say no. Some are afraid to speak up or are concerned about suffering negative consequences if they speak up. Others are so shocked and embarrassed that they cannot bring themselves to face the actor, much less speak to him or her. I don't want to mislead you. Some actors will not stop, even if you say no, but many will. If you are afraid, have someone with you when you speak to the actor. It's a good idea to have someone with you for moral support when you object to the behavior, but it is not required.

Objecting to the behavior serves another purpose. If you complain to your employer or sue your employer, the fact that you objected is good evidence that you did not welcome the behavior. The company and the courts can look at other factors to determine whether you did not welcome the behavior. Still, nothing is as good as a clear no.

The next step is to ask for what you want: the promotion, the raise, the removal of a negative evaluation, the transfer, or whatever you were denied. Many people forget this step. They may say they don't like the behavior, but they fail to ask for what they want. You must make a request.

Don't invite the actor to lunch, dinner, drinks, coffee, a private location, or party to discuss things or to smooth things out. I've spoken to many targets who have been advised by friends to meet the actor outside of work for a quiet conversation to work things out. Don't do it. Don't invite the actor anywhere. This should be obvious and self-explanatory, but you'd be surprised how many women think that a quiet talk over cocktails will straighten things out, or that they'll just make things worse if they exclude the actor from their annual Fourth of July picnic. Don't approach someone socially who is treating you offensively for any reason. You will be tempted to do this at some point. Women often want to repair broken relationships, so they do things to make things better and to avoid hurting the other person's feelings. This will not work to stop the behavior. The invitation will imply that you enjoy the behavior. You will only encourage the actor to continue.

Inviting the actor to do anything is a mixed message. People hear what they want to hear. An invitation means you want to spend more time with the actor and that you liked or welcomed the behavior.

Down the line in the company's investigation, or in a lawsuit, your invitations will be used as evidence that you welcomed his behavior. A later investigation or lawsuit will uncover the fact that you voluntarily socialized with the person after the offensive behavior. Any social invitation can be used to prove that you had positive, not negative, feelings toward the actor and that you welcomed the earlier behavior.

No matter how tempted you are, avoid social contact of any kind with the actor.

3. Tell someone you trust about what happened.

It is important to tell someone you trust what happened. You do not have to go through this alone. Confide in a family member, close friend, or trusted coworker. Allow that person to support you, even if all that person does is listen to you. Other forms of support include assisting you in reading and understanding the sexual harassment policy, encouraging you to speak to the actor (see #5) or the responsible supervisor (see #6), or reading any accounts of the events you may write.

Choose the person who will support you carefully. This must be someone who will validate your feelings and support you to take the appropriate actions. If your best friend tells you to forget what happened and move on with your life, find someone else to support you.

4. Get a copy of your employer's sexual harassment policy and read it.

It is critical that you read your employer's sexual harassment policy, even if you were given a policy when you were hired or participated in sexual harassment training. Employers sometimes update their sexual harassment policies. Be sure to get the latest version of the policy and read it. Pay particular attention to the definition of sexual harassment, the procedure for complaining, and the name of the person who is authorized to receive complaints. Underline or highlight certain sentences if you need to.

The point of this is to be clear whether the behavior you are concerned about falls within the definition. It's possible you will discover that the behavior that concerns you doesn't fall within the definition. It doesn't matter. You have the right to set your own boundaries and ask people to respect them, even if the behavior does not fall in the definition of sexual harassment.

5. Keep a diary of everything that happens, including names, dates, events and how you feel.

Write down everything that happens and date each entry, starting at the point when you first sense something is wrong. This includes everything the actor said or did, everything you said or did in response, and how you feel. Include the names of people who saw or heard what happened. Keep your diary at home. Do not keep it at work or on your office computer. Materials you keep at work can disappear or be found by others. Also, anything you save on your employer's computer belongs to your employer, not to you. In the event that you lose your job, you could also lose all your records of what happened.

I'm not suggesting that you obsess over the behavior. Your diary will serve several purposes. It will focus your attention on the fact that something is happening. It will help you to be present and to focus on the facts. (If no one is doing anything to you, which is possible, the diary will also reveal this.) Seeing the facts in writing will reassure you that you are not imagining things. If and when you report the unwanted behavior to the responsible person at your company, he or she will ask you what happened. With your diary in hand, you will be prepared to answer questions of who, what, when, and how. Emotions and the passage of time may make it difficult to recall the details.

I am always surprised how many people came to me with complaints of sexually harassing behavior who cannot remember even the approximate dates on which they were pinched, groped, or insulted.

When your employer investigates your complaint, the gathering of facts will be a critical part of the investigation. Having the facts will assist the company in its investigation of your report. Having the names of people who witnessed the events will make the investigation go much more quickly.

Finally, if the actor gives a different story, your diary will support your version of what happened. Most sexual harassment occurs in private. There are typically only two witnesses, you and the person about whom you are complaining. The employer will have to determine whose version to believe. Your diary will be what the law of evidence refers to as "contemporaneous record" of the events; that is, a record made at the time the events occurred. It can be used as evidence that your story is truthful and accurate.

6. **If the behavior continues, report the behavior to the person in the company who is responsible for receiving sexual harassment complaints (the responsible supervisor).**

The employer's sexual harassment policy will state the type of behavior that is prohibited and the procedure your employer has established for reporting of sexual harassment. You will find it under the heading "How to make a complaint." Speak to the person listed in the procedure as the person responsible for receiving complaints. If you don't feel comfortable speaking to that person, send that person a written note. Then call the head of your human resources department and ask to speak to someone else.

This is the point where many people get stopped. It can be intimidating to consider reporting someone through official channels. It is a serious step, but if the behavior doesn't stop after you make the request, it is a necessary step.

You do not have to report the behavior to your supervisor, especially if your supervisor is the person about whom you are complaining.

Next to confronting the actor, people find reporting the offensive behavior the most difficult thing to do. It's difficult for several reasons. Many people think they won't be believed or won't be taken seriously. Others believe nothing will be done. I have heard many women who say they don't want to ruin the actor's career. They just want to be left to work in peace. They are concerned the actor will be fired or otherwise punished in a way that will ruin his or her career. They are afraid the employer or the actor will retaliate against them if they submit a report.

Rather than encouraging employees to report sexual harassment, so-called "zero-tolerance" policies sometimes discourage reporting. This kind of policy usually imposes a remedy or punishment that outweighs the seriousness of the behavior. In Chapter 13, I describe alternatives to zero-tolerance policies that tend to encourage employees to report inappropriate behavior.

Most employers don't communicate to their employees how they have responded to sexual harassment complaints, leaving employees to assume they do nothing.

Most sexual harassment can be stopped effectively by telling the actor to stop the behavior. Some actors won't be stopped by a simple no. You want to be clear who and what you are dealing with. Those who won't stop are the jerks, the dummies, the princes, and the predators.

The jerks do not care whom they offend or how their behavior affects other people. Jerks entertain themselves at the expense of others. Jerks know their behavior is offensive, and they don't care. What they want to do is more important than how it affects others. You can often identify a jerk by certain characteristic responses: "What's the big deal?"; "Don't be so sensitive."; "Can't you take a joke?"; or "What are you going to do about it?" Jerks often travel in packs and require an audience of other jerks. A jerk will not respond to your objection. You will have to report a jerk.

The dummies are simply oblivious to their own actions and their effect on others. Dummies are often socially inept. Don't make the mistake of thinking a dummy is stupid. Dummies can perform brilliantly in their work, but they are under-developed socially. Dummies often mimic the behavior of others in an attempt to be accepted. Dummies can control their behavior, but they don't process social interactions well. Dummies will respond to punishment. You have to report a dummy.

A prince is a very successful executive or manager who thinks he can get away with anything. A prince is a jerk with a big salary. You have to report a prince.

A predator is a supervisor or manager who makes sexual demands of a subordinate or who ignores a subordinate's requests to stop offensive, intimidating, or hostile sexual behavior. A predator knows what he or she is doing, knows it is inappropriate, knows the damage he or she is doing, and does not care. A predator is often sufficiently clever or powerful to manipulate the target and the employer. Sometimes, the predator is a partner or the business owner. Predators can also be identified by their tendency to make threats and characteristic responses such as "No one will believe you," "If you report this, you'll be sorry," or "I'm in charge here, so there's nothing you can do." You have to report a predator and will likely have to sue the employer to stop a predator.

The law requires your employer to take prompt, corrective action when you report behavior that could be sexual harassment. At the very least, your employer must investigate to determine what happened. The sooner your employer knows about your problem, the sooner you can get action. Most incidents of sexual harassment are not reported. Until you tell someone, nothing can be done. Make sure that you make your report to the proper person. Consult your company's equal opportunity policy or the human resources department to get the name of the person designated to receive complaints. You can also make the report to your supervisor, unless the supervisor is the person you are complaining about or that person's best friend. The law does not allow your employer to require you to report incidents of sexual harassment to your supervisor.

If the person you complain to says there is nothing they can do, then ask who can do something. Your supervisor should have received training in what to do when an employee complains about being sexually harassed, but many companies still do not provide this training. You must be prepared to identify the proper person or office yourself.

Once you have identified the person responsible for receiving your complaint, make an appointment to meet the person face to face. Insist on having an appointment within 48 hours. If the person you contact cannot meet you within 48 hours, ask to meet with another authorized person. You should be able to meet the person in his or her office, in your office, in your supervisor's office (if the supervisor is supportive), or at a location away from the work site.

Tell the responsible supervisor the facts of what happened and how you feel.

You will probably be afraid and upset, but when you meet the responsible person you must stick to the facts of what happened and when it happened. The more specific you can be, the better. Bring your diary and refer to it. The person who receives your complaint may give you the opportunity to put your complaint in writing. If so, take the opportunity and submit the written statement within the time requested. Ask someone you trust to review the written statement before you turn it in.

If the person you speak to is unwilling to promise what will happen next and by when, continue to contact people in your organization until someone agrees to do something specific, even if you have to call the president of the company. Keep a record of everyone you speak to, when, and what they say.

It will be up to you to follow up with the responsible supervisor to make sure someone takes action following your initial conversation. Once you have spoken with the responsible person, ask what will happen next and by when you will hear from the officer again. If you don't hear from the responsible person on the date promised, call back on that date and ask:

- Have you done anything with my complaint?
- What happens next?
- Will my report be investigated?
- Who is responsible for conducting the investigation?
- What happens after that?
- Who makes the final decision?

- When and how will I be notified about the results of the investigation and the final decision?

Many employers' policies offer an opportunity for counseling. You should feel free to take advantage of this service. Counseling should assist you to understand the employer's policies and procedures and how to deal with the person whose behavior concerns you. A counselor may even assist you to evaluate the behavior and whether it falls within the definition of sexual harassment. A counselor may even offer to assist you in deciding whether to make a formal complaint. Whatever the counselor says, the decision whether to make a complaint is your decision.

7. Cooperate with the investigation.

At some point, you will be contacted for an interview, probably early in the investigation. The person conducting the investigation will ask you questions and may interview you more than once. Answer the questions and submit copies of any documents you have, such as letters, e-mails, or poor evaluations. Never relinquish original documents. Bring a set of copies with you, or make copies before you leave the person's office. (See Chapter 11 for what happens in the investigation.)

8. Complain to an external agency.

If you cannot identify a responsible person to receive your complaint, if the responsible person does not return your call, or if the responsible person says that your complaint will not be investigated, don't threaten to sue. Complain to an external agency.

You do not have to wait for your employer to complete its investigation to seek outside help. Agencies at the federal, state, and local level are authorized to investigate complaints of unlawful employment discrimination. The federal agency is the Equal Employment Opportunity Commission. Most states and local governments also have antidiscrimination laws and agencies that enforce those laws. You can locate the contact information for these agencies on your state and city governments' Websites or in the government listings in the telephone book.

These external agencies have strict deadlines for making complaints. The deadline for making a complaint to the Equal Employment Opportunity Commission (EEOC) is 180 days (six months) from the date of the discriminatory act you are complaining about. Do not wait longer than 180 days to contact the EEOC. There is very little anyone can do if you miss this deadline for filing a complaint. If you don't want to pursue a complaint, you can always change your mind and withdraw the complaint. You can also amend, or change, your complaint to add additional facts.

The time for filing a complaint with an external agency continues to pass while you are deciding whether to complain to your employer. The time continues to pass while your employer is considering your complaint. I can't emphasize too much the importance of acting within the prescribed time if you are going to complain to an external agency.

Some state and local agencies have different deadlines for filing complaints. The New York State Division of Human Rights and the New York City Commission on Human Rights will accept complaints up to one year after the behavior.

These agencies cannot order your employer to do anything. The staff of the agency will make findings as to whether there was "probable cause to believe that there was unlawful discrimination," or there was "no probable cause to believe there was unlawful discrimination." This means the agency will gather facts and determine whether you were probably discriminated against.

The external agency's staff will contact your employer for information for facts about what happened. If the agency's staff thinks you were probably discriminated against, they will attempt to engage in conciliation. Conciliation is an attempt by the external agency to get you and your employer to come to a friendly agreement in which both of you are satisfied. Conciliation usually leaves both you and your employer getting less than you hoped to get.

Conciliation is voluntary and both parties, you and your employer, must agree. You do not necessarily need a lawyer to complain to an external agency. But do not sign a conciliation agreement without consulting a lawyer.

9. Contact a lawyer and decide whether to sue your employer.

You do not want to have to sue your company. A lawsuit is the last resort. If you cannot find anyone in your company to promise to investigate, this is a good time to call a lawyer. If you have complained to an external agency, and the agency asks you to agree to or to sign something, this is a good time to call a lawyer.

The decision to sue your employer is a critical decision. A lawsuit can involve years of expense, meetings, answering questions, and reviewing documents. Only you can decide whether a lawsuit is worth it. There are no general guidelines for deciding whether to sue. There are, however, several things to think about. If you answer yes to all of the following questions, suing your employer may be the course you would take. If you answer no to any of these questions, it may not make sense for you to sue:

- Have you talked to a lawyer who specializes in sexual harassment cases?

- Is there something that you want that you were not given or offered: a denied raise or promotion, a negative evaluation removed from your file, removal of the person you are complaining about from your work unit, reinstatement to a job from which you were fired, or specific change in how employees are treated?

- Do you have emotional support from your family and friends?

- Do you have the financial resources to support yourself while the lawsuit is pending?

A lawsuit is a difficult undertaking for a plaintiff in an employment discrimination suit. Not only can a lawsuit go on for years with no result, you will be fighting a large or small corporation that has the financial and legal resources to sustain a legal battle. Many people have abandoned a good legal claim and been better off for it. On the other hand, the law provides a remedy for unlawful employment discrimination, and you are entitled to seek justice in the courts. The plaintiffs in the early sexual harassment cases I described in Chapter 1 had no reason to believe they would win, based on past legal decisions. But win they did, and I have no doubt that their lives were forever changed by the outcome. Our lives certainly were changed. But only they can tell you whether it was worth it.

Federal law is not the only basis for a lawsuit against your employer or the person you are complaining about. State law also provides remedies for such actions as assault and intentional infliction of emotional harm, known as personal injuries, and can carry large monetary awards. If you decide to sue, have a thorough conversation with a lawyer about all the possible actions that you might have against your employer and others. Also, be very clear about the costs of a lawsuit and how those costs will be paid. Some lawyers will take your case and allow their attorneys' fees to be paid by the employer if you win a lawsuit. There are also other costs to consider, aside from the attorney's fees.

What to Do If You Are Accused of Sexual Harassment

"Wait just a minute," said the engineer sitting in the front row in one of my workshops. "It sounds like you are trying to change our behavior. You can't change this kind of behavior. It's human nature."

"Let's take a look at that," I asked. "Were you born designing computer circuits?"

"No," the engineer replied.

"And how many academic degrees do you have in engineering?"

"Three," he replied. "One from Stanford and two from MIT."

"Think of it this way," I said. "You have learned to design a computer circuit, and you can learn to treat your coworkers with respect."

• • •

My aim is to change everyone's behavior, men, women, supervisors, and the organizations that employ them. I am teaching people to alter the quality of their experience at work. When the behavior changes, the experience changes. This is one paper bag we cannot "think" ourselves out of. The men who speak with me about sexual harassment complain about four things:

1. Oversensitive women.
2. No clear-cut rules about what is acceptable behavior
3. Vengeful women who lie to get men in trouble
4. Having to watch everything they say (no more compliments, joking around, or friendly pats on the back).

No matter how careful you are, the likelihood is that, at some time or another, someone will accuse you of discriminating against him or her in some way. Unless you are within a few days of retirement, someone will probably accuse you of sexually harassing him or her at some time in the course of your working life. If you are a supervisor or manager, it cannot be avoided. It goes with the territory.

Being accused of sexual harassment is serious business. An accusation can lead to workplace discord, scandal, discipline, and even termination. It can cause negative publicity for the company, industry-wide rumors, bad feeling, and lost productivity. A formal complaint obligates the employer to investigate the allegations and take prompt corrective action.

Once the target submits a formal complaint, no matter how understanding the employer is or how conciliatory the employer represents the complaint procedure to be, the process becomes adversarial. The actor does not want to be found to have sexually harassed the target, the employer wants to protect itself, and the target wants to stop the behavior and get whatever he or she may have lost as a result of the behavior.

I advocate dealing with the situation as it occurs and to avoid getting to the formal complaint stage. The actor, that is, the person whose behavior is being complained about, has the opportunity, and sometimes many opportunities, to accomplish this.

You can be accused of sexual harassment when:

- The target complains to you directly about your behavior.
- Someone else, a fellow employee or supervisor, expresses concern about your behavior.
- The person who is responsible for receiving complaints notifies you someone has filed a formal complaint against you.

Almost no one ever thinks they have sexually harassed anyone. The opportunity to shift the action is in the moment the action is happening or immediately thereafter. You have to pay attention. You have to encourage the people you work with to tell you what offends them. You have to be willing to respect others' wishes and personal boundaries. Rarely will someone admit to wrongdoing, apologize, and promise never to do it again.

For the most part, nearly everyone who is accused responds in one of these ways:

- "I didn't do it."
- "I was kidding around."
- "The person complaining is too sensitive."

- "That's not what I meant."
- "It wasn't that serious."

Here are the six actions to take when someone accuses you of sexual harassment:

1. Listen to the target's concerns and take them seriously.

2. Educate yourself about the policy and procedure, and encourage fellow workers to tell you what behavior is acceptable and unacceptable.

3. Avoid the behavior a target says was unwelcome, declined, or expressed a concern about.

4. Determine what support and advice you need and get it.

5. Evaluate your options.

6. Reach an amicable solution

1. Listen to the target's concerns and take them seriously.

We do not usually call it a complaint when someone tells you directly or indicates in some way that they do not like what you are doing. The key to dealing with an accusation of sexual harassment is recognizing the target's communication for what it is: a complaint. Whether it is a mild expression of dislike or a request to stop, take it as a complaint. Many accusations get to the formal complaint stage when the actor continues unwelcome behavior, despite expressions of dislike. You will miss the opportunity to address the target's concerns unless you are paying attention, are interested in the target's experience, and take the concerns seriously.

2. **Educate yourself about the policy and procedure, and encourage fellow workers to tell you what behavior is acceptable and unacceptable.**

Most of us think our behavior is just fine. We tend to think everything we do is welcome. Educating yourself about the policy and taking an objective look at whether your behavior might offend someone will allow you to make necessary adjustments. Then you can begin the process of learning from your fellow workers what kinds of behavior they do not welcome.

3. **Avoid the behavior a target says was unwelcome, declined, or expressed a concern about.**

Do not intentionally repeat unwelcome behavior or behavior that offends, upsets, intimidates, or humiliates others.

4. **Determine what support and advice you need and get it.**

If you are concerned about a situation, it is smart to get help. Your manager, human resources manager, or Equal Employment Opportunity officer, can assist you to address the situation before it becomes difficult or a complaint is filed against you.

5. **Evaluate your options.**

If a formal complaint has been filed against you, you may have to get legal advice. A complaint can result in discipline, and you want to protect your rights. If no complaint has been filed, you still have the opportunity to shift the course of events. You always have the option to find out specifically what the target's concern is, even if you think you did not violate the policy. Even if the target files a complaint, cooperate with the investigation and make sure the investigator gets your full story. Otherwise, a decision will be made without the benefit of any information from you.

6. Reach an amicable solution.

Come to some agreement about how you and the target are going to work together. A sexual harassment complaint does not mean the end of the world. It does not necessarily mean you are going to be fired. Before a final decision has been made on a formal sexual harassment complaint, there is always the possibility to reach an amicable solution.

If someone expresses a concern to you about your behavior toward someone else, follow the same six steps. In addition, do not try to talk to the target about the complaint. If possible, find out from the person who brings you the concern exactly what you did that was unwelcome, but do not have this conversation with him or her alone. Consider having your manager or someone from the human resources department or Equal Employment Opportunity office accompany you. If you cannot get this information from the person who mentioned the concern to you, tell your manager or someone from the human resources department or Equal Employment Opportunity office that someone may have a concern about you and you want to get it resolved. Do not, under any circumstances, try to convince the target that your behavior was not offensive, humiliating, or intimidating. It is the target's experience that is relevant, not yours.

Your objective in the conversation is to acknowledge that you heard the communication, to clarify what behavior was unwelcome, to promise not to do what was complained about, and then to keep your promise. You could schedule a follow-up conversation with the person who spoke to you to assure yourself that the target has not expressed any additional concerns. Document all conversations with a memorandum to the file, and send your manager a copy.

If the person who is responsible for receiving complaints notifies you a complaint has been filed against you, your options shift dramatically.

- Read the complaint. The written notice will include a copy of the target's complaint, stating what the target alleges you did.

- Call the person who sent you the notice and get clear information about the procedure and what happens next.

- Talk to people who may have witnessed the situations described in the complaint. Ask them what they recall happened and whether they are willing to speak on your behalf. You will give the investigator the names of the people who were present.

- Cooperate with the investigation. The investigation will address whether you did what was alleged, whether your actions constituted sexual harassment and, if it was sexual harassment, what would be appropriate corrective action.

If you did not do what is alleged in the complaint, you will need witnesses who can tell the investigator what happened. If you did what was alleged in the complaint, be prepared to agree not to do it again and to accept some form of discipline. The investigator will recommend corrective action, which can include discipline. Your attitude during the investigation may influence the investigator's recommendation about discipline.

The corrective action will be designed to ensure the behavior does not happen again. Your willingness to avoid the behavior in the future may influence the recommendation and any subsequent discipline.

Do not discuss the complaint with the target or try to convince him or her to withdraw the complaint. Any attempt to influence the target to withdraw her complaint could be a new violation and subject you to harsher discipline.

The following is an example of how these steps can work in practice:

> Joe supervises Clara, a dispatcher for a delivery service. From time to time, he comes to her workstation for various legitimate purposes. Joe is a long-time employee. Clara has worked for the company for three months and is up for her 90-day review. Clara sits at a workstation with a computer screen and keyboard. On his visits to oversee Clara's work, Joe leans over her shoulder to see the entries on her computer screen. He occasionally reaches over and types on her keyboard to view data about the day's transactions. Clara feels Joe stands too close to her and, sometimes, when he reaches over to type on her keyboard, his hand brushes against her shoulder or hand. Clara has never said anything to Joe about it.
>
> On a particular visit, Joe reached to type on Clara's keyboard and his hand brushed again her breast. Clara adjusted her body away from his hand, but neither of them said anything. Clara felt uncomfortable, but figured it was a mistake. Neither she nor Joe mentioned the incident.
>
> A few days later, Joe visited Clara's workstation, and once again, his hand brushed lightly against her breast. Again, she adjusted her position away from his

hand. The following day, Joe leaned over to view her computer screen. He said, "Wow. Your hair always smells so good." Clara did not respond.

Uncomfortable, concerned, and unsure what to do, Clara called in sick the following day. The next day she said to Joe, "It made me uncomfortable when you touched me the other day. I need you to be more careful when you check my work. I don't want to make trouble. This job is important to me, but if you touch me again, I'm going to complain to your manager."

Joe said, "You're a smart girl, and I'd like to see you do well here. Threatening me is not the best way to do that."

Clara complained to Joe's manager that Joe insisted on leaning over her when he reviewed her work, touched her breast on two occasions, and made a sexual remark to her. Joe did not recommend that Clara be retained as an employee. His report of her performance included the following recommendation: "Clara is punctual, works quickly, has mastered our systems, and produces excellent results. Unfortunately, she is not a team player, and she resists supervision. In the long run, this will hamper her growth and the unit's productivity." Clara failed her 90-day review and was fired. The day she was fired, she filed a sexual harassment complaint with the human resources officer responsible for receiving sexual harassment complaints.

Joe responded that the complaint was ridiculous, that he once said Clara's hair smelled nice, and he never tried anything with her.

Joe's actions at Clara's workstation, taken individually, probably do not constitute sexual harassment. All actions are taken in context, and actions that may not be sexual harassment when viewed individually could be sexual harassment when viewed together and in the context of everything that happened. When Joe stood close enough to Clara to make her uncomfortable, it was not sexual behavior in itself. We would have to look at whether he supervised male employees by leaning over them. For example, we would want to know whether Joe stood this close to Clara, but not other employees. We would want to know whether he leaned over female employees, but asked male employees to step aside while he viewed their computer screens. That would tell us whether he had a gender agenda.

The first time his hand brushed against her breast could have been accidental. The second time may also have been accidental. So far, probably still no sexual harassment. However, when Clara shifted her body away from his hand, it was a clear indication that the behavior was not wanted. This was Joe's first opportunity to shift his action.

The second time Joe's hand touched her breast and she shifted her body away from him, she gave a second clear and unmistakable signal the behavior was unwanted. This was Joe's second missed opportunity.

Joe's final action at the workstation, commenting on the smell of Clara's hair, was not only gender specific, but also continued the unwanted behavior. This was the third missed opportunity.

Joe's next two mistakes were to ignore Clara's request that he stop the behavior that concerned her and to threaten her job. He threatened her with losing her job when he said, "You're a smart girl, and I'd like to see you do well here. Threatening me is not the best way to do that." It may have been indirect and thinly veiled, but it is reasonable to conclude that he was threatening her with negative consequences if she continued to complain. Supervisors sometimes make comments like this without appreciating the full impact. His reaction to Clara's complaint was personal and without any regard for his employee's sensibilities or his employer's possible exposure to legal liability. He was preserving his authority over a new and powerless employee.

Finally, Joe gave Clara a negative performance review based on her having expressed a concern about his behavior and caused her to be fired. He penalized her in retaliation for rejecting his unwelcome actions in supervising her.

• • •

The repeated unwelcome sex-specific behavior, the threat, the negative performance review, and the loss of her job constitute sexual harassment. The unwelcome sexual advances, together with any one of the three consequences would have been enough to constitute sexual harassment. If Clara files a sexual harassment complaint with an outside agency or sues her employer, she is likely to prevail.

Let's say Joe had missed all the signals. He still could have thanked Clara for coming to him with her concern, asked her exactly what he had done to make her uncomfortable, and said he would take care to avoid touching her in the future. In addition, he could have given some thought to how he would avoid the behavior in the future. To aid him in thinking about what to do, Joe should educate himself about the employer's sexual harassment policy. Even if he has had sexual harassment training, he should pull out the employer's sexual harassment policy and read it. He could look to see how the policy applies to his actions.

Joe should have advised Clara to speak to the person designated to receive sexual harassment complaints. He should also have reported his conversation to that person and request support to resolve the situation quickly and amicably.

Joe could then decide how he is going to make sure he does not touch Clara in the future. He could ask her to step away from her computer while he views her screen. He could make arrangements to be able to view her screen remotely from another computer or rearrange her workspace so there is room for him to view her screen and touch her keyboard without standing behind her. He could ask her to type on her keyboard instead of doing it himself. He should never again refer to how she smells.

Joe should have disclosed the conversation to his supervisor and asked for advice on how to supervise Clara without making her uncomfortable. The manager could have made suggestions or had Joe visit the Equal Opportunity Officer for advice on how to proceed. Joe should share with Clara the actions he has taken and will take, and he should document those conversations.

If you have been accused:

- ☑ Listen to the target.
- ☑ Educate yourself.
- ☑ Avoid the behavior.
- ☑ Determine what support and advice you need.
- ☑ Evaluate your options.
- ☑ Reach an amicable solution.

• • •

A note about employees who complain after they have been fired

It is very common for employees who have experienced sexual harassment or other forms of discrimination to complain only after they have been terminated. Many people hold back from complaining, not wanting to rock the boat, make trouble, or risk retaliation. Once they have been fired, they no longer have anything to lose. Often, a discrimination complaint is the only way available to challenge the termination. This presents a real challenge for employers. Employers want their termination decisions to stick, and the complaint looks like the desperate action of a disgruntled employed. It is important for employers to remember that these complaints could have merit. Employers often take these complaints lightly, and they do so at their peril.

It is critical that employers take all complaints seriously, especially when a negative employment action has been taken. Taking a complaint seriously does not mean the employer must assume the complaint is valid. It means investigating the complaint promptly and thoroughly, making a determination that is consistent with the employer's policy, and taking appropriate action.

What a Supervisor Should Do When an Employee Complains

Quick! You are a supervisor, and an employee tells you he or she has been sexually harassed. What should you do?

The Quick! List

Here are the nine things a supervisor should do if an employee complains about possible sexual harassment:

1. Listen without interrupting.

2. Find out whether there is a threat to the employee's safety.

3. Tell the employee what you will do.

4. Tell the employee that a sexual harassment policy exists, and give him or her a copy of the policy.

5. Answer questions about policy and process.

6. Acknowledge feelings.

7. Ask questions to clarify the story, and take notes.

8. Tell the employee what you will do.

9. Immediately report the matter to the Equal Employment Opportunity officer (EEO) for your organization or other person responsible for receiving sexual harassment complaints.

If you are a supervisor, you probably will first encounter sexual harassment when an employee comes to you to complain. You will expect him or her to ask about vacation time, a raise, or a work-related issue. You may find this type of encounter a little uncomfortable, but you will tend to feel prepared for the conversation you expect.

Instead, she says: "I have a problem that I need to talk to you about. I'm not sure there's anything you can do about it. Mack and I have been working on the Acme account for three months now and, well, it's hard to explain. We started working late. Sometimes we order in Chinese food. He sits too close to me and says things. I don't know what to do. I can't work with him anymore."

She may not use the words "complaint" or "sexual harassment." Nonetheless, she may be complaining about being sexually harassed. You are now in the role of the responsible supervisor, and you have a legal obligation to act. The supervisor's actions at this moment are the most critical actions anyone acting on behalf of the employer will take in the process of addressing the possible complaint.

If you are the employee, you are probably upset, embarrassed, worried, angry, or all four. You probably expect that your supervisor will do nothing.

How the supervisor responds in this moment is critical. What the supervisor does now, at the initial contact, will largely determine whether the employee will sue the company down the road. The employee's first contact might not be a personal visit. The target may contact you by telephone, e-mail, letter, or some other communication, such as a note on your desk. You must ask the employee to meet with you as soon as possible. Schedule to meet with the target immediately, the same day. If that is not possible, you must make yourself available to meet within the next 24 hours. If you are not available, arrange for someone else appropriate to meet with the employee. These conversations are awkward and uncomfortable, and it is natural to want to put it off.

Delay can be deadly. The target expects you to do nothing. Delaying the meeting is the equivalent of doing nothing. Once you do nothing, you have verified all his or her worse beliefs about you and your company: you don't care, and you won't help him or her. Whatever you do down the road is unlikely to convince the target otherwise. If you and the company move slowly at the outset, every subsequent delay seems that much longer. Investigations take time and require patience on the part of everyone involved. Delay at the outset is like being late for the first meeting with someone. It's hard to recover.

Some of these actions may seem to be overkill. After all, you are busy, and you won't be making the final decision about this situation. Some of the actions listed below are legally required. Others are obvious. Some, such as explaining your role in the process and promising what actions you will take, could save your having to learn a hard lesson. Your company cannot legally require subordinates to report sexual harassment to their immediate supervisor. A subordinate may come to you, anyway. An employee who works for another supervisor could come to you for help. It is important to be prepared.

1. Listen.

Allow the employee to tell you everything that she has to say about what happened, without interruption. Do not open the door for other visitors, do not answer the telephone, and do not fiddle with papers.

It is natural to become embarrassed in this conversation. After all, this may sound to you like a personal problem between two employees. Worse, it might sound like a scandal that is being dumped in your lap. In addition, the subject is sex, a subject that makes most people at least a little uncomfortable.

The employee is embarrassed, too. If he or she is not embarrassed, then he or she is angry or upset. In either case, the employee needs and wants someone to listen to what he or she has to say; so it is your job to listen without interrupting. If the employee uses personal pronouns (such as he, she, they, or I), you may interrupt only to clarify the identity of the person or persons about whom he or she is speaking. You may also interrupt to ask when the actions took place. Otherwise, do not interrupt the employee. After he or she has finished talking, ask whether he or she has anything else to tell you. You would be surprised how often an employee will give you key information at the end of the story.

This is not necessarily the time to take notes and to document the story. That will come later. The first objective is to get a clear view of the situation. The second objective is to make sure the employee is not in any danger. The third objective is to get all the information you need to act responsibly on behalf of your employer. The fourth objective is to assure the employee that you will take action in response to the concerns.

2. Find out whether there is a threat to the employee's safety.

Ask: "Are you afraid for your safety? Has this person threatened you or hurt you in any way?" Ask the employee what happened to make him or her concerned and immediately call the person who is responsible for security. That person will know what to do. Sometimes, the employee will be in real danger or the person he or she is concerned about will be crazy or dangerous. If so, you have both a possible security issue and a possible sexual harassment issue. You want to know up front if someone is looking for this employee with a firearm, for example, especially because the person is sitting in your office. Once any security issues have been addressed, you can move on to the sexual harassment issue.

3. Tell the employee what you will do and what he or she can expect to happen next.

In all likelihood, the employee will either expect you to do nothing to help him or her or will demand immediate action. In either event, you must tell the target what you will do and what he or she can expect to happen next. If you do not know what will happen next, tell the employee that you will find out and contact him or her with the information. Then, get the information and contact the employee.

Most people don't like to make promises, especially if they don't know what is going to happen or if another person is involved. You are not going to promise that the actor will be punished, and you are not going to promise any particular outcome. You can promise what you will do. You can also promise that the company will follow its sexual harassment policy. If you cannot promise these two things, then you have a problem.

This part of the conversation can go something like this: "I appreciate your coming to me with your concern. The first thing I am going to do is to make sure you have a copy of the sexual harassment policy. Then, I'm going to ask you a few questions and take some notes, so that I am clear about what you've told me. My responsibility under the sexual harassment policy is to report this conversation to the Equal Opportunity Officer, which I will do today. Under the policy, he is required to contact you within 10 days and complete the investigation within 60 days. I will follow up with him to make sure he has contacted you. If you don't hear from him within 10 days, you have the right to write a letter directly to the president of the company. You can also feel free to contact me, if you write to the president of the company and he doesn't respond."

Several years ago, I attended a workshop in sexual harassment for college administrators. The workshop panelists were five administrators who worked directly for presidents of major universities. The moderator asked what they would do if a student complained that their boss, the president of the university, had asked her to have sex with him. The panelists spoke about whether the best course of action would be to confront the president directly or to seek advice from a member of the Board of Trustees. Not one of the five experienced administrators mentioned a policy on sexual harassment or their universities' procedures for dealing with discrimination complaints. They all agreed that this was a special and difficult matter and that it required discretion and creativity.

Even experienced supervisors may be tempted to abandon or forget the company's sexual harassment policy in order to deal with what appears to be a special situation, just as these college staffers indicated they would have. Every complaint about sexual harassment will appear to be special. Someone has been accused of conduct that could conceivably cause a scandal if it were to be made public. An employee is upset. The supervisor can bring order and certainty to an emotional situation by consulting and following established procedures. It is critically important to follow the procedures in the sexual harassment policy.

If you are the employee, you should bring the organization's sexual harassment policy with you and refer to it during the meeting.

4. **Tell the employee that the company (or agency) has a policy that prohibits sexual harassment, and ask him or her whether he or she has read it. Whether or not he or she has read it, provide a copy of the policy. (Most sexual harassment policies will have similar provisions.)**

    Tell him or her:

    -   Unwelcome sexual advances that affect his or her work or create a hostile, offensive, or intimidating work environment are prohibited by the employer's policy.

    -   A designated person will investigate the facts and, when his or her story is verified, appropriate action will be taken. Give the employee the name, title, office location, and telephone number of the person who is responsible for the investigation. It is possible but unlikely that your company does not have a sexual harassment policy. If that is the case, tell him or her that you will contact the legal department or the head of the human resources department.

- You will ask the employee a few questions and take notes to make sure that you understand the facts, just as he or she told them.

- There is a range of possible outcomes, including disciplinary measures and corrective actions, if there has been a violation of the sexual harassment policy.

- As far as possible, you will keep the conversation confidential, but you will have to share the information he or she will give you with the EEO officer or another manager in order to address the concern.

5. Answer the employee's questions about policy and process.

It is important to ask whether the employee has any questions about the policy or how the process works. This may feel too legalistic and formal to talk about at this moment, but you must establish a clear understanding with the employee about what you can and cannot do. Do not promise to take care of the situation or to discipline anyone. The accused employee has a right to be heard before any irrevocable actions are taken.

6. Acknowledge the employee's feelings.

It will help both you and the employee if you remember and respect the words that he or she uses to describe how he or she is feeling. If the employee has said that he or she is embarrassed, say, "I understand that you feel embarrassed."

The employee often will say that he or she doesn't want you to do anything, but that he or she just needed to tell someone. The employee is probably concerned about having revealed a very private matter and his or her very personal feelings. He or she doesn't want to be the subject of company gossip, even well-meaning gossip. The employee has probably been told that nothing will be done. Speaking to you is an act of trust. Explain to the employee again that you will keep his or her report confidential, to the extent that it is possible to do so. Explain further that the law requires that the employer must take prompt action regarding any reports of sexual harassment. Assure him or her that you will inform only those persons who must know in order for appropriate action to be taken. Tell the employee that your first responsibility is to inform the EEO officer. The EEO officer will advise him or her whether others in the company must be informed.

Your responsibility as the supervisor (or as the person responsible for receiving sexual harassment complaints) is to the employer and not to the complaining employee. Keep in mind that the purpose of your actions is to protect the complaining employee from the alleged harassment, to preserve the rights and confidentiality of everyone involved, to protect other employees who may be affected by the alleged behavior, and to protect the employer from legal liability that could result from your failure to bring the complaint to the attention of the proper person.

In a case I investigated, a supervisor called me about a problem. She had promised four employees who had approached her for help with someone who was sexually harassing them that she would keep their identities confidential. This was a big mistake. I had to remind the supervisor that she was responsible to the organization, not the employees. Her job was to allow me to address the problem on behalf of her employer. I told her she had to go back to the employees and tell them she had made a mistake. As a supervisor, she had to disclose their names to the responsible officer and explain to them that no one else would be told, unless it was necessary to address the problem. The company cannot address a problem if the supervisor keeps secrets, even if the employee wants to maintain confidentiality.

7. Ask questions to clarify the story and take notes.

Once you have followed steps one through six, the employee understands the context of your conversation and the purpose of your questions. Have him or her tell you the first and last names of the person or persons whose behavior he or she is concerned about, when and where the behavior took place, and what, if anything, he or she did in response to the behavior. Ask only enough questions to be able to report the conversation accurately. Take notes.

Most sexual harassment policies require the supervisor to report the incident to another person immediately. Some policies prohibit the supervisor from conducting an investigation or asking the employee any questions. This works when the employee says, "I've been sexually harassed. I want action." The supervisor must ask enough questions to know whether the situation involves sexual harassment. I have seen policies that prohibit the supervisor from asking any questions at all, in an apparent effort to make sure the supervisor doesn't conduct an investigation. In my view, overly rigid policies that don't allow the employee to have a conversation with the person she approaches for help tend to leave the employee alienated. Imagine going to your supervisor's office for support in dealing with a sexual harassment problem and being told, "I am not allowed to speak with you about this. Fill in this form and call the number on the top." Some policies work this way.

In any event, you should follow your company's policy. If there is any conflict between anything I am suggesting here and your organization's sexual harassment policy, follow the policy. Then, consult the Equal Employment Opportunity officer or your legal department.

8. At the conclusion of the meeting, once again tell the employee what you will do and what he or she can expect to happen next.

Give a specific time by when you or someone else will contact him or her. This is your opportunity to provide leadership and certainty. Promising to take specific actions within a specific time will also give you some structure in an emotional situation.

9. Immediately report the conversation to the EEO officer or other person responsible for receiving and investigating complaints of sexual harassment.

Do not delay in reporting the conversation to the responsible person. Your initial conversation with the employee is not an investigation. Do not determine whether the situation is a case of sexual harassment; you are not qualified or authorized to assess the facts. The best you can do is to conclude that, if everything the employee told you is true, then this could be a situation involving sexual harassment.

You might not want to report the conversation. Let's say you know the other person and you find it unbelievable that he or she could possibly have sexually harassed anyone. Let's say you conclude that the employee must be overreacting or that a potentially scandalous situation needs to be kept quiet. As a supervisor, if you delay reporting the conversation to the person who is responsible for receiving and investigating sexual harassment complaints, you could cause your company to lose a lawsuit. You may also leave a troubled employee with no other recourse but to take you and your company to court.

As the employee, or target, you should expect and insist on some action within the promised period of time. If you are the actor, you will not know this conversation has happened until the person conducting the investigation contacts you.

What Employers Can Do

The employer's responsibilities are to make reasonable efforts to prevent sexual harassment, to have an effective complaint procedure, and to take prompt action to correct sexual harassment it knows about or should know about.

Relatively recent changes in the law have affected the employer's responsibility for the actions of supervisors. An employer is now liable when an employee rebuffs a supervisor's unwanted sexual attention and then, as a result, the employee has an economic loss because of an employment decision the supervisor made. A court will treat the supervisor's actions as the employer's actions, as though the board of directors had passed a resolution directing that the sexual harassment be carried out. The employer will be responsible for the harassment, even if the employee did not report the harassment and if the employer did not know about the supervisor's actions. If the allegations are proved, there is no defense.

Employers who want to avoid liability for sexual harassment in the form of official decisions by its supervisor's actions need to take almost heroic measures to make sure supervisors do not make decisions about hiring, firing, wages, leave time, and other economic aspects of work in connection with unwelcome sexual behavior.

The supervisor is likely to be the first contact within the employer's organization for an employee who believes he or she has been sexually harassed. The supervisor is also likely to be the person whose actions are the source of concern. Careful attention to the role of supervisors and how supervisors respond to situations that may involve sexual harassment are two important aspects of the employer's responsibility for dealing with sexual harassment.

In addition to the primary responsibility to avoid sexually harassing employees, an employer can avoid liability for sexual harassment by coworkers who are not the target's supervisor if:

- The employer exercised reasonable care to prevent and correct promptly any sexually harassing behavior.

- The target unreasonably failed to take advantage of any preventive or corrective opportunities provided by the employer or to avoid harm otherwise.

Exercising reasonable care to prevent and correct promptly any sexually harassing behavior includes:

- Having a policy that prohibits sexual harassment.

- Having an accessible effective complaint procedure that employees are likely to use.

- Training all employees in the policy and how to use the complaint procedure.

- Taking prompt corrective action on all complaints.

If an employer fulfills these responsibilities and the employee has not experienced any tangible loss as the result of the harassment, the employer can avoid liability for the harassment, even if the employee did not use the employer's complaint procedure. This is critical because most sexual harassment is never reported.

Have a policy that prohibits sexual harassment

An effective policy will state unambiguously that sexual harassment is prohibited in the organization, define sexual harassment, and include who is covered by the policy. Employees need to know that the actions of all employees, suppliers, agents, contractors, and consultants are covered.

The policy will also acknowledge that harassment of someone of the same sex is also prohibited. As discussed in Chapter 3, there is no requirement that the behavior be the result of sexual attraction. There is no requirement that the actor be homosexual if the target is the same sex as the actor.

The policy should define sexual harassment, describe sexual harassment in a manner that employees can understand, and promise that the employer will act promptly on all complaints. The policy should use the definition provided by the Equal Employment Opportunity Commission or in state or local law. It is helpful to provide examples of sexual harassing behavior in the policy, although that is not required.

The policy should include the kinds of remedies that are available and the possible consequences of engaging in sexual harassment. Avoid such language as "zero tolerance" and "will not be tolerated." The employer's actions indicate much more credibly the organization's level of commitment to the policy than language that scares people.

Having a policy includes distributing the policy to all employees. In a large company, the policy needs to be in writing, and the employer needs to monitor that every employee actually receives it. In smaller companies where the owner communicates regularly with all the employees and there is relatively little employee turnover, communicating the policy verbally can meet the legal requirement. I recommend putting the policy in writing, regardless of the number of employees, so there is no mistake about what is prohibited.

Have an accessible complaint procedure

A complaint procedure states how to submit a report of sexual harassment. An accessible complaint procedure is easy to use. It includes the name, title, office location, and telephone number of the person designated to receive complaints, how to submit a complaint, by when a complaint must be submitted, assurance that all complaints will be investigated, by whom and by when the investigation will be completed, the title of the person who will make the final decision as to what actions, if any, will be taken, and by when the results of the investigation will be communicated to the parties.

An accessible complaint procedure is easy and welcoming for employees to use. An accessible complaint procedure states specifically that an employee does not have to submit a complaint to his or her supervisor. This is because the supervisor may well be the person who is the subject of the complaint, or the supervisor may already know about the behavior and have done nothing about it.

An accessible complaint procedure makes the person designated to receive complaints easy to find. If the designated person is busy or out of the office, it provides that someone else will be available to receive a complaint. An accessible complaint procedure also takes into account common reasons people may be reluctant to report sexual harassment.

Some employees may be uncomfortable speaking to a particular person. Designate more than one person to receive complaints and include as designated persons males and females, people of different ethnicities, and people of different ranks within the organization.

Others may be concerned that people will know they are making a complaint. Allow the complaining employee to meet with the designated person on "neutral territory," out of the office, or in a location that is different from the designated person's office or the complaining employee's work location. You cannot promise complete confidentiality. There are people in the organization who must be told about the complaint for appropriate action to be taken. You can, however, offer a degree of privacy when the person makes the complaint.

An employee may be uncertain about what to do or what will happen. Allow an opportunity for the employee to find out what his or her options are for dealing with the situation, what reporting involves, and how to deal with the actor while the complaint is being investigated. Someone should be able to counsel employees about how the complaint procedure works and what they can do about particular situations.

An accessible complaint procedure inspires confidence. It actually works. Complaints are investigated and investigated promptly. Employees know the procedure works. If it is common knowledge that nothing ever happens when an employee complains, employees will be reluctant to use the procedure, and the procedure is not accessible. While employers may be appropriately reluctant to disclose the outcomes of particular complaints, they need to find ways to inspire confidence in their procedure. An employer might distribute annually to employees the number of complaints that were brought and investigated during the year and the number of complaints in which corrective action was taken.

I share more about creative approaches in Chapter 13.

Train all employees

The law does not explicitly require sexual harassment training for employees, and only a few states, including California, Connecticut, and Maine require sexual harassment training. The typical purpose of sexual harassment training is to explain to employees what behavior is prohibited as well as to convey the employer's commitment to enforcing the policy. While most people know and understand that sexual harassment is an issue in the workplace, not everyone understands that the law applies to them. Training serves the additional purpose of leaving everyone certain that the policy does, indeed, apply to them, and encourages employees to report incidents of sexual harassment.

Effective sexual harassment training alters values and behavior, in addition to delivering information. Some managers have never been told it is unacceptable to exploit employees for their personal agendas. In some industries, notably entertainment, finance, and computer technology, young managers can rise to great power in their 20s, having never had to manage their own behavior. Those who generate high revenues for the employers and are the owners, themselves, may never have been called upon to manage their behavior or be responsible for anything other than their level of production. Effective training changes what is important to managers and supervisors like these, leaves them valuing the experience of their fellow workers, and makes them aware of how their behavior can affect other employees and create a potential risk of liability for both their employer and for themselves.

Many employers use online sexual harassment training services. Online training is less expensive and avoids the need to schedule employees for group sessions. I do not recommend online training for the simple reason that supervisors must hear directly from someone they respect that they may not sexually harass their subordinates. They can easily assume that the organization is not serious about a policy that does not warrant a face-to-face meeting.

Some managers and employers find it bizarre that I recommend encouraging employees to report sexual harassment. The fact is that unless the employer knows about violations of the policy, it is difficult to do anything about them. Encouraging reports gives the employer an edge in knowing what is happening in his or her organization. Encouraging employees to report sexual harassment also tends to counteract the widespread perception that employers are not interested and will not act on complaints.

The policy must have the explicit support of the head of the organization, whether that is a CEO, commissioner, administrator, mayor, or other top officer. Unless the policy is promulgated by and signed by that top person, it is unlikely to be taken seriously.

Take prompt corrective action

Corrective action is not just about discipline. Corrective action is reasonably calculated to remedy the target's loss, to stop the harassment, and to prevent it from happening again. For example, if a target received a poor performance evaluation because of sexual harassment by his or her supervisor, corrective action would include removing the poor evaluation from the personnel file. Corrective action would also include disciplining the supervisor. Discipline can include sexual harassment counseling, suspension, loss of supervisory status (demotion), or termination. Decisions about discipline should take into account the likelihood the actor will do the same thing again.

Discipline for sexual harassment violations can be a controversial subject. Some people believe that all violators should be terminated. Progressive remedies, that is, the application of less severe remedies for less severe violations and more severe remedies for more severe or repeated violations, are more effective. Some employers find themselves having to counteract the negative publicity that often follows a report of sexual harassment in an effort to prove their commitment to punishing violators. A common reaction, firing anyone who violates the policy, can backfire. Overly harsh discipline, or discipline that employees perceive to be overly harsh, tends to discourage reporting. Overly harsh one-size-fits-all penalties also discourage actors from acknowledging the behavior and committing to respect the policy in the future. Why confess what you did if the inevitable result is termination? Progressive remedies are more consistent with the idea of corrective action.

Corrective action has to be prompt. In general, corrective action should be taken within a week of the report. This means that the complaint needs to be investigated, a decision made, and the corrective action taken within that time. In one case, a delay of 13 days was considered to be too long. If the investigation is likely to take longer than a week, the employer should take some intermediate action. The idea is to both protect the target and to avoid liability, if it is later concluded there was sexual harassment. Intermediate action can include separating the actor and the target to avoid daily contact, temporarily removing the target from the actor's supervision, confiscating any offensive material, or other actions calculated to stop the behavior.

When implementing permanent or temporary corrective action, avoid imposing an additional burden on the target. Because the actor is often a higher-ranking male, it is usually easier and more beneficial to the employer to move or to transfer the target, who is often a lower-ranking female. As a result, the actor stays put in the interim, doing his work as usual, while the target's work life is disrupted.

One challenge that employers face is how to stay ahead of changes in the law. Many employers tailor their sexual harassment prevention programs to do exactly what the law requires and no more. The best way to stay ahead of changes in the law is to do more than the law requires. Chapter 13 addresses how employers and employees can work together to change the aspects of workplace culture that spawn and perpetuate sexual harassment.

Investigations: Who Is Telling the Truth?

The investigator has the sometimes difficult task of uncovering what happened. A big part of the investigator's job is to get the people involved to talk and, more importantly, to tell the truth.

It is easy for the investigator to assume that others, especially professional colleagues, will cooperate in the investigation because they understand the complaint process and appreciate the investigator's good intentions. In this very personal area of discrimination law, the investigator probes employees' feelings and motives, their sense of humiliation and loss of dignity, and the sometimes sensitive issue of performance evaluations. Getting to the truth can be a delicate matter. One of the investigator's tasks is to avoid making the investigation itself the issue.

How the investigation is conducted and how the investigator treats the employees involved can determine not only whether the investigation gets to what happened, but also whether employees will be willing to cooperate in this and future investigations.

Karen, the smart, serious and energetic Equal Employment Opportunity officer for a large organization, took her responsibility for investigating discrimination complaints very seriously. An expert in discrimination law, she understood the importance of following procedures and conducting a prompt, thorough investigation. She did not always enjoy the often difficult and tedious work of interviewing employees after she received a complaint. She was concerned that her decisions would affect the lives of the people involved.

One morning Mark, one of her colleagues, approached me in an agitated state. He said, "I need your help. I know that Karen is doing her job, but she is making the people in my department crazy. She's scheduled appointments with a number of people and told them that someone accused them of race discrimination. She started asking questions, and now everyone is scared. They don't want to talk to her without me in the room with them. I can't get my work done. I don't have time to sit through hours of interviews. She's like a bull in a china shop. Can't you talk to her?"

I asked him whether he had told Karen about his concerns. He had not. He said that he knew that if he spoke to her it would look as though he was trying to influence the investigation or protect his people. He said he was willing to cooperate and to encourage his subordinates to cooperate. He said he knew that Karen had to do her job and that the complaint had to be investigated. He did not want to stop her, but the way she was going about it was causing problems. He came to me, he added, because he knew I would be fair.

I told Karen about Mark's concerns and asked her how the investigation was going and what problems she had encountered. Karen had interviewed the complaining employee and informed the accused employee about the complaint. She had, as the employer's procedures required, contacted the complaining employee's immediate supervisor, that person's supervisor, and two or three coworkers in the same unit. She told them that a complaint had been made and offered to let them read the written complaint. She had also scheduled meetings to interview each of them about the facts and asked the supervisor against whom the complaint was made to submit a written response. She had followed the agency's procedures precisely.

She said, "They aren't acting like professionals. They should know that I have to get the facts in a case before I make a decision. They gave me justifications and told me they did not discriminate against the employee. They are acting as though I should just make the decision based on what they tell me. I'm having trouble getting them to tell me what they did."

She continued, "They all want the department head to be present when I talk to them, which makes it difficult. He doesn't have all day to sit in on these interviews."

I shared with Karen my observations of people when they are accused of discrimination against a fellow employee. People may know intellectually that there must be an investigation before the decision can be made as to what happened; but at the moment they find out they have been accused of a wrong, particularly a moral wrong, such as using their supervisory powers to discriminate against a subordinate, what they know intellectually becomes less important than what they feel personally.

Most people vigorously deny the charge, whether or not they committed the act of which they are accused. They feel also that the investigator must believe that the charge could be true, or they would not be subjected to questioning. They feel afraid of what could happen to them if the charges are believed. Finally, they doubt whether the investigator will, or even can, reserve judgment until after all the facts have been gathered.

After sharing this perspective with Karen, I advised her: "You have to establish the context for your investigation with the accused employee and each witness. People don't know what to expect. You have to tell them exactly what you are going to do and how you are going to approach your decision. If they don't trust you or the process, they won't tell you anything useful."

As I told Karen, when you make the initial contact, you have to tell the accused employee that:

1. A complaint has been made and, at this point, it is only a complaint.

2. You are required to investigate the facts.

3. You will not draw any conclusions about the facts until after you have completed all of the interviews and have read his or her response, if he or she offers one.

4. You understand that being accused of a serious violation of the law is very troubling, but that you will need to know everything that he or she can tell you about what happened.

5. As the investigator you have specific questions, but you want to hear anything he or she wants to add or tell in the interview.

6. You will hold everything that you learn during the investigation in confidence, and you will share information only with the people in the agency who must know the facts in order to act on the complaint or help in the investigation.

7. You will be fair and objective in your review of the case.

8. You will answer any questions that he or she has about the process or your responsibilities before you proceed with the interview.

9. You didn't intend to disrupt the work of the office, but you must complete your report within a certain number of days.

10. You are willing to schedule the interview and follow up interviews at convenient times.

11. He or she is entitled to have a copy of the complaint and a person of your choice accompany you to each meeting [as was required by the employer's sexual harassment policy].

12. You will submit a report of the investigation and recommendations for corrective action to the decision maker who will decide whether action with be taken.

As she left my office, Karen said she had not read what I had shared with her anywhere else and suggested I write a book.

Several days after my conversation with Karen, her previously upset colleague, Mark, said to me, "I don't know what you did, but Karen changed her approach and everyone has calmed down. Thanks a lot."

What is an investigation?

An investigation is the process of gathering facts, determining whether the alleged behavior occurred, concluding whether the behavior is sexual harassment, and recommending what corrective action should be taken, if any. An investigation can be as simple as interviewing the complaining employee and concluding that the behavior complained of is not sexual harassment. An investigation may also be complex. It can include interviews with many witnesses, follow-up interviews of witnesses, gathering and examining documents, visits to locations where the behavior occurred and consideration of previously verified complaints against the same person.

The quality of the investigation, including the respect with which the investigator treats witnesses, the professionalism with which the investigator conducts interviews, and the integrity of the investigator in keeping appointments and other promises, all influence whether employees are willing to bring complaints and trust the process.

Who is telling the truth?

Once the investigator has gathered the facts, he or she must decide whose version of what happened is more believable. This aspect of the investigation is called assessing the credibility of witnesses. Contrary to popular belief, trained investigators have lots of tools for determining what happened when there are no witnesses to the alleged sexual harassment other than the target and the actor or actors. The issue of who is telling the truth is no more of a problem in sexual harassment investigations than it is on other types of cases, such as thefts, where determinations are made every day, despite the frequent lack of eyewitnesses.

Judges have a lot of experience deciding who is telling the truth. They consider factors such as the witness's demeanor (how the witness acts and speaks), inconsistencies in the witness's story, and whether other witnesses corroborate any part of that witness's story. Investigators weigh the same kind of evidence to help determine whether a witness is telling the truth in sexual harassment complaints.

Sexual harassment complaints appear to require more proof because if the complaint is believed, it could derail the career of a high-ranking person. Also, the higher-ranking person is often perceived to be more important to the organization than the lower-ranking person, which can be a motivation for disbelieving the complaint.

How to conduct a thorough investigation

The employer is responsible for making sure investigations are conducted promptly and thoroughly. The following steps will guide you in assuring thorough, objective, and organized investigations. If you are making or considering a complaint, these steps will give you an idea of what to expect. If you have been accused of sexually harassing a fellow employee, these steps will help you to understand the process and how to cooperate with the investigation.

- ☐ **Carefully select and train the person who will conduct the investigation.**

Make sure the people who are designated to investigate complaints support the policy, have sufficient time to devote to investigations, and are trained in equal employment opportunity law and investigation procedures for discrimination complaints. You would be surprised how many people tell me their employer's complaint process is "a joke" because the person designated to receive sexual harassment complaints is the office's biggest sexual harasser.

Select someone who has at least several years' experience investigating employment discrimination complaints. The Equal Employment Opportunity Commission provides training for investigators, as do many state government's equal employment opportunity agencies and private consulting companies. Consider engaging an outside law firm or employment discrimination consulting service to investigate complaints.

▣ **Review the complaint log on a regular basis.**

The complaint log records basic information about every complaint. Reviewing it will tell you instantly whether you are responding promptly to complaints.

▣ **Get all the available facts.**

The investigator's ability to get all the available facts will depend largely on whether people with the information cooperate and have confidence in the complaint process. The investigator should speak to everyone who might have knowledge about what happened, including people the target may have told about the behavior near the time it happened, and review every document involved. Sometimes it is important to visit the locations where the behavior occurred. If the person who conducts the investigation is also the person who receives the initial complaint, have that person follow the instructions in Chapter 9.

⊡ **Reserve judgment until the investigation has concluded.**

Reserving judgment is surprisingly difficult to do. While it is impossible to avoid having opinions, reserving judgment means willing to be wrong about initial opinions, and questioning everything.

⊡ **Investigate every element of the complaint.**

The first and obvious questions are "Did the behavior happen?" and "Was the behavior sexual?" The investigator must also ask "Was the behavior unwelcome?" If the target suffered a loss, the investigator has to confirm there was a loss and whether the employment decision resulted from the target's rejection of the behavior. If the complaint involves hostile environment harassment, the investigator must ask, "Did the behavior unreasonably interfere with the target's work performance or create an intimidating, hostile, or offensive work environment?"

Some of these questions are factual. The effect of the behavior on the target relates to the target's subjective reaction. The investigator must ask the target how he or she felt. The investigator may be tempted to accept statements such as, "We were just kidding around" or "Can't she take a joke?" as justifications for the behavior. The actor's humorous intentions are not relevant to how the behavior affected the target and whether it was sexual harassment.

The investigator has to form independent opinions and not rely on the conclusions and opinions of witnesses. Others' reactions do not necessarily determine whether the complaining employee experienced sexual harassment. It is tempting to dismiss a single employee's concerns if other employees put up with, were not bothered by, or were amused by the behavior. Frequently, employees will have become so accustomed to sexual behavior or language at work that it doesn't bother them anymore, or they may have given up on any possibility of changing the situation. A new employee may react differently to behavior than people who have been around for a while. A woman may react differently to behavior that doesn't offend men in a previously all-male workplace, or a man may be offended by behavior that doesn't offend the women in a previously all-female workplace. Employees may perceive behavior differently when they come from different cultural or ethnic backgrounds.

The investigator's focus needs to be on the effect of the behavior on the target's work performance and the target's work environment.

☐ **Document everything.**

List in an investigation log every interview, telephone call, e-mail (sent and received), and document collected in the course of the investigation. The decision-maker must be able to make a good-faith determination that there is good cause to believe that the behavior occurred. He or she must determine that the investigator's conclusions are based on a reasonable investigation and supported by substantial evidence. This is possible only if the investigation is fully documented.

☐ **Conclude, to the best of the investigator's ability, what probably happened, that is what the evidence says most likely happened.**

The investigator's job is to determine not what actually happened, but what probably happened, based on credible or substantial evidence. The investigator does not have to prove there was sexual harassment beyond a reasonable doubt. Thinking the investigation will resolve what happened with absolute certainty can sidetrack an investigator. The investigator did not see what happened, and it is rare to get consistent stories even when many people witnessed the behavior. The best service the investigator can perform is to conclude, based on a thorough investigation, substantial evidence, and credible support, whether there is good reason to believe whether the actions in the alleged in the complaint happened. The decision-maker must read the investigator's report and question how and on what basis the investigator assessed the witnesses' credibility.

Special Types of Complaints
Certain complaints can be especially perplexing.

Late complaints

What should the employer do if an employee complains many months, or even years, after the harassment allegedly occurred? The employer should investigate every complaint of sexual harassment. It can be tempting to think, "This is coming too late for us to do anything about it." This employee's late complaint could signal to the employer that "there is a fox in the hen house." If other employees' complaints about the same actor were ignored or mishandled, this late complaint could be the employer's first opportunity to remedy the situation. The employer cannot know the facts or take appropriate action unless there is an investigation.

Even if the behavior has stopped, the actor may have gotten the message that there are no consequences for his behavior and moved on to another target. If there is no investigation of the late complaint, the employer could later be held liable for having failed to take action on behavior it knew about or should have known about.

Complaint follows an earlier relationship or affair

What should the employer do if the target complains about someone with whom he or she has been involved sexually or romantically? The employer should investigate any complaint of unwelcome sexual advances, even if the target and actor had a previous personal relationship. A target who welcomed sexual advances at an earlier time has the right to say no at any time.

The Top 10 Reasons Sexual Harassment Investigations Miss the Point

1. **Delay.** The investigation starts too late, after witnesses' memories have faded, evidence has disappeared, the target has become discouraged, or witnesses have formed alliances.

2. **Ignoring procedure.** The investigation does not follow the employer's complaint procedure.

3. **Legal errors.** The investigator does not assess correctly whether the behavior is sexual harassment.

4. **Jumping the gun.** The investigator forms an opinion too early.

5. **Poor quality investigation.** The investigator ignores proper investigative procedures, such as speaking to all witnesses, seeking all relevant evidence, documenting interviews, and preserving all the relevant evidence or is not skilled in interviewing.

6. **Misplaced altruism.** The investigator tries to resolve the situation or to help the parties "get along," instead of investigating the complaint and submitting a report.

7. **Inconsistent intentions.** The investigator is serving another objective, such as validating the decision-maker's preconceived conclusion or making an example of the actor.

8. **Conflict of interest.** The investigator has not disclosed a conflict of interest, such as bias toward one of the parties, personal knowledge of the facts, or personal disagreement with the policy.

9. **Employer interference.** The decision-maker or someone else in authority insists the investigator complete the investigation prematurely, directs a particular result, or makes a decision without reviewing the investigator's report.

10. **Something else came up.** In cases where the target is in danger of being harmed by the actor, everyone forgets about the sexual harassment complaint while taking action to protect the target or while criminal charges are pending against the actor.

Remedies

It is critically important that both employees and employers, not just lawyers, be aware of the remedies that are available and appropriate in sexual harassment cases. Targets often want only to stop the harassing behavior and to undo unfair employment decisions. Knowing the range of available remedies and disciplinary actions will assist employers in making appropriate demands for corrective actions.

Employers are already aware of the potentially devastating costs of sexual harassment litigation and the need to prevent sexually harassing behavior. A prompt and appropriate remedy in response to a complaint may avoid a lawsuit altogether. A prompt and appropriate remedy may prevent a finding of liability if the complaining employee sues.

Many targets do not report incidents of sexual harassment because they are concerned that there will be no remedy, or because they fear the remedy will be too harsh. Employers should create and announce a series of progressive remedies, beginning with minor remedies for minor infractions and serious remedies for serious or continuing violations. Progressive remedies can actually encourage reporting.

The remedy must be designed to accomplish two objectives. It must attempt to make the target "whole," or to put the target back in the same position he or she enjoyed before the sexual harassment occurred. This can involve undoing a discriminatory personnel decision, paying lost wages, or arranging a previously denied transfer. The remedy must also ensure that the sexual harassment will not reoccur. This will usually require taking some disciplinary action against the actor. Often, especially in instances where the harassment was hostile environment harassment, the target will have suffered little or no economic loss. Nonetheless, insofar as it is possible, the remedy must be designed to accomplish both objectives.

When announcing or publishing possible progressive disciplinary actions, the employer should characterize them as guidelines, allowing for flexible application of progressive discipline in particular situations. In practice, it is important to apply similar discipline for similar behavior.

Internal remedies

The severity of the behavior has to be taken into account.

- Verbal harassment, such as offensive jokes and sexual comments, may be appropriately addressed by additional mandatory training and a warning that repeated harassing behavior will result in more serious discipline.

- Repeated or serious unwelcome touching, such as touching the target's private areas, should be addressed by suspension or termination.

- Supervisors who threaten employees with negative personnel actions or extort sexual favors from subordinates with the promise of positive personnel actions should be terminated.
- Supervisors who engage in hostile environment harassment should be terminated or should lose their supervisory status.

In all cases, a second violation should have a more serious consequence.

Employers can feel pressure to impose the maximum penalty for every violation. People tend to believe that anything less than termination amounts to no discipline at all. People tend to laugh when the corrective action requires an actor to attend counseling or sexual harassment training. The fact is that appropriate and effective sexual harassment training can have a profound and permanent effect on a behavior.

I have conducted mandatory sexual harassment training that was imposed on accused employees as an aspect of the corrective action following sexual harassment cases. I personally conducted the one-on-one training that lasted for several hours, tailored the training to emphasize the employee's particular behavioral lapse, and made it crystal clear that employees would be fired if they ever repeated the behavior. The training sessions were both memorable and effective.

The tendency to impose maximum penalties for every violation tends to discourage targets from reporting incidents of sexual harassment. Many targets are not interested in ruining the actor's career. They just want the behavior to stop. The likelihood the actor will be terminated can discourage them from reporting.

Employers should have a range of appropriate remedies available.

Judicial remedies

Some of the judicial remedies that are available in discrimination cases, which include sexual harassment cases, are back pay, front pay, punitive damages, attorneys' fees, and a court order instructing the employer not to discriminate. Back pay compensates the plaintiff for wages that were lost because of the discrimination. Front pay is wages the plaintiff is entitled to until he or she can be placed in an appropriate new job. Punitive damages, which are limited to $300,000 in federal cases, are awarded only when the discrimination was intentional discrimination and if the defendant acted maliciously or with "reckless or callous indifference to the federally protected rights of others."

Courts can also order employers to implement prevention programs, such as sexual harassment training, counseling, improved complaint procedures, and wide publication of its antidiscrimination policy.

Attorneys' fees, which can also be substantial, are intended to encourage plaintiffs in discrimination cases to pursue their rights in the courts. Attorneys' fees can include costly expert witness fees.

σ • σ • σ • σ • ♀ • ♀ • ♀ • ♀

Part III

• • •

Creating a
Culture
of
Respect

Preventing Sexual Harassment
Before It Happens

Basic prevention activities are usually enough to eliminate much of the employer's risk of liability. Issuing an antidiscrimination policy and implementing prompt corrective action when a sexual harassment complaint has been verified are a good start. Preventing sexual harassment before it happens will involve more than the basics. It will involve employers, management, supervisory personnel, and other employees working together to alter the workplace culture. Fundamental changes in how we interact can dramatically expand our ability to prevent sexual harassment at its source.

Challenge #1:
The Inevitability of Sexual Interest

As I said in Chapter 1, whenever people (whether they are men and women, men and men, or women and women) are in close proximity, there will be sexual attraction and sexual advances. Of course, not all sexual harassment involves sexual interest. Even when sexual harassment involves sexual interest, it typically also involves an abuse of power.

It can be an individual supervisor abusing his or her supervisory power to coerce a subordinate. It can be a persistent coworker abusing his or her power over someone who is reluctant to or unskilled at standing up for herself or himself. It can be an unrestrained group using group power to intimidate an individual.

Some employers try to avoid the potential sexual harassment that can come from inappropriately expressed sexual interest by imposing nonfraternization policies, that is, prohibiting sexual and romantic activity among workers.

In some cases, having a nonfraternization policy means the employer doesn't have to determine whether workplace sexual behavior was voluntary, consensual, welcome, or unwelcome. Once the employer discovers there was sexual or romantic activity, the employer can discipline the employees who violated the policy. Any actor who claims the target welcomed, voluntarily engaged in, or consented to the sexual activity is actually admitting to violating the nonfraternization policy.

A nonfraternization policy is easier to enforce than is a sexual harassment policy, but it tends to yield two unacceptable results. First, the target and the actor can both be disciplined for violating the policy, even though the target may have been coerced into participating. Second, targets will be more likely to hide or deny that sexually harassing behavior occurred because they fear the consequences for themselves.

Strategies: Prohibit sexual and romantic activity between supervisors and subordinates and between trainers and trainees during the supervisory or training relationship. Employers can also encourage responsible decision-making and behavior.

Challenge #2:
Ineffective Communication

Preventing sexual harassment in the workplace requires effective communication. Unfortunately, people do not communicate effectively. We don't say what we mean, we don't mean what we say, we don't ask for what we want, and we don't pay attention when other people are speaking. Prevention activities with any hope of success have to include targets making it known when behavior is unwelcome and requesting that the unwelcome behavior stop. They will also have to include actors paying attention to targets' requests and stopping behavior when asked.

Strategies: Encourage employees to discuss personal boundaries, and what is acceptable and unacceptable behavior. Encourage employees to speak up when they experience unwelcome behavior. Train employees to stop sexual behavior unless they receive an unmistakable, direct, and welcoming response.

Challenge #3:
Fear

Targets fear the employer will do nothing, impose an excessively punitive remedy, or retaliate. Actors fear being disciplined for innocent behavior. Employers fear big lawsuits.

Strategies: Publicize the employer's preventive measures and response to complaints. Help employees to separate actors who respond to a request to stop from actors who ignore a request to stop. Discipline persistent violators.

Challenge #4:
Abuse of Power

Abuse of individual power

Many supervisors produce excellent business results, but have poor interpersonal skills and little appreciation for their subordinates' needs.

Abuse of group power

Groups engage in behavior that individuals would not. Examples include teasing, foul language, grabbing, groping, and other behavior commonly termed "locker room" or "shop floor" behavior, that sometimes accompanies the introduction of women into all-male or male-dominated work environments. Abuse of group power sometimes accompanies the introduction of men into all-female or female-dominated work environments. The worse thing an employer can do is to accept unlawful behavior as uncontrollable.

Abuse of organizational power

Abuse of organizational power occurs when organizations avoid investigating complaints of sexual harassment and ignore the well-known harassing behavior of one or more high-level individuals. Strategies include complaining, making a record, and appealing to outside agencies, including the courts. Abuse of organizational power is the most insidious, because it leaves employees discouraged and without any support within the organization. Abuse of organizational power is also the biggest source of costly awards and settlements.

Strategies: Reward managers and supervisors who comply with and champion the employer's antidiscrimination policy. Implement training and discipline to discourage the kind of group thinking and group acting that leads to the abuse of group power. Encourage observers to communicate their disapproval to group leaders. Check into departments and offices that are hotbeds of complaints, resignations, disappearances, requests for transfer, and excessive sick leave. Include gender sensitivity and effective treatment of complaints as specific indicators when evaluating the performance of managers and supervisors. Quantify the cost of sexual harassment, and treat it as an avoidable expense that cuts into business profitability. Eliminate sexual activities, such as strippers and other overtly sexual entertainment, from business events. Prohibit holding business meetings at strip clubs and all-male clubs.

Challenge #5:
Gender Stereotyping and Other Forms of Sex Discrimination

Gender stereotyping and nonsexual gender discrimination encourage sexual harassment. Gender discrimination includes using derogatory language toward women; joking during performance evaluations of women; having women take minutes at meetings; and using women as surrogate wives to serve coffee, buy personal gifts, organize parties, and take lunch orders. Gender stereotyping also includes having women employees concentrated in secretarial and assistant positions, using female employees as lures for business dinners, and having few women in upper-management positions.

Strategies: Upgrade language about women, include women at all levels of the organization; avoid using women as surrogate wives. Model appropriate behavior. Promote and hire women into important positions.

Challenge #6:
Workplace Situations That Are Ripe for Sexual Harassment and Complaints

Expect the number of discrimination complaints to rise following annual conferences, holiday parties, and other office celebrations. These situations, where people let down their guard, drink excessive amounts of alcohol, and feel less pressure to conform to normal workplace rules, are ripe for sexual harassment.

Discrimination complaints, including sexual harassment complaints, also tend to increase right after performance reviews and layoffs.

Strategies: Send a memo before the event reminding employees about the sexual harassment policy. Meet with managers and supervisors before the event to remind them the policy applies during the event. Arrange transportation home and escorts for employees after the party. Make confidential counseling sessions available after the party to allow employees to debrief and plan how they will communicate about party behavior they now regret.

Carefully review performance evaluations and the basis for poor performance reviews. Train supervisors in how to communicate the bad news. Fire or lay people off early in the week and early in the day, not on Friday at 4:30 p.m.

Unique Environments:
Schools, Colleges, and Universities;
the Military; and the Church

Every workplace environment has different characteristics that distinguish it from other workplaces. Educational institutions, military organizations, religious institutions, and government agencies have unique characteristics that warrant special attention. People who work, study, and participate in these settings face unique problems when they confront and address sexual harassment.

People who work in these environments have the same rights to equal employment opportunity, including protection from sexual harassment, as do employees in traditional business environments. As employers, these organizations have the same responsibilities to their employees as other employers have: to issue a policy prohibiting sexual harassment, to avoid sexually harassing their employees, to make reasonable efforts to prevent sexual harassment, to provide an effective way for employees to complain, to investigate complaints and to take prompt corrective action. The preventive measures in Chapter 13 can all be applied in all these organizations.

Educational institutions have additional legal obligations to protect their students from unlawful discrimination, as required by Title IX of the Civil Rights Act of 1992, as well as state and local laws. Religious institutions have legal obligations to protect their worshippers from sexual abuse under various criminal codes.

This book is not intended to address all abusive sexual behavior in all contexts, such as sexual assault, rape, date rape, domestic abuse, incest, child abuse, and crimes against women in wartime. Sexual harassment can take the form of criminal behavior. Sex crimes, whether or not they are sexual harassment, are symptomatic of a similar disregard for others and cannot always be completely separated from workplace sexual harassment in practice.

Some workplace characteristics can increase the likelihood sexual harassment will occur and make it more difficult to detect and prevent. Sexual harassment in religious institutions, which tend to be insular, secretive, highly male-dominated, and intensely protective of their clergy, is difficult to expose. Military organizations have some of the same characteristics and are subject to a system of military justice, making it difficult to expose the level of sexual harassment that exists. In addition to sexual harassment, physical assault, rape, demoralization, isolation, and retaliation for speaking out are critical issues facing women in the military.

I urge employers to design creative preventive programs that address the particular issues of their work environments and take advantage of their organization's particular strengths and resources. The basic features of most policies will be similar, but there is a lot of freedom when it comes to complaint procedures, investigative protocols, training and education, and opportunities for dialogue. This chapter will focus on colleges and universities.

College and university faculty typically do not think of themselves as employees in the strict sense. Employees in colleges and universities tend to think of themselves more as comrades on a common quest, supporters of a noble mission, or members of a tight-knit family, than as employees. Faculty often regulate their own work hours, do much of the work at home or without direct supervision, and are regularly given credit for work they do in the larger community. As a result, faculty often think they can do whatever they want to do, without consequences. Most college and university faculty members now understand that sexual harassment laws apply to them.

Colleges and universities foster unusually close relationships between faculty members and between faculty and students. They encourage a degree of dependence, affection, camaraderie or collegiality, explicit sharing of values, and personal trust that tends to blur the distinction between supervisor and subordinate. A big challenge for colleges and universities is having faculty members understand that the sexual harassment policy applies to close mentoring relationships, such as graduate students they employ as research assistants and young professors they are shepherding toward promotion.

Without the kind of job mobility often found in business, powerful superiors in these settings, such as principals, department chairs, and deans, can remain in place for years. Employment protections, such as tenure for college professors, can make it difficult to discipline employees who violate rules that prohibit sexual harassment.

In a residential campus setting, expansive open campuses, facilities that are open around the clock, and late-night activities create safety issues that don't exist in the typical business environment. Young people, most of whom are away from home for the first time, experimenting with their new freedom, and very trusting, need special guidance.

The same principles apply to developing effective strategies for eliminating sexual harassment in educational institutions as they apply in other employment settings. Because they are in the education business, colleges and universities have a unique opportunity to create programs that educate their employees and students to develop dynamic new models for relating across gender lines and for having regard for how their behavior impacts others.

In 1982, I drafted an innovative sexual harassment policy and prevention program for Hunter College of the City University in New York. The college's sexual harassment policy, procedures, and prevention activities had to address the actions and concerns of faculty members, administrators, staff, and students, any of whom could be targets or actors. The procedures had to work for faculty-on-faculty harassment, faculty-on-administration harassment, faculty-on-student harassment, administration-on-faculty harassment, administration-on-student harassment, and student-on-student harassment. Complaints brought by students, faculty, and staff required different decision-makers in different offices. The faculty and administrative staff were unionized, and we had to safeguard their specific procedural rights.

The first objective was to make the procedure simple. In close consultation with the president of the college, the staff, and the faculty leadership, we decided to have one central receiving point for all complaints. That way, it would be easy for a target to know where to go, without having to determine in what category and office his or her complaint belonged.

The second objective was to give people a choice of people with whom they could speak. An important consideration was that some students might relate better to another student. We created a committee (called a "panel") that included men, women, people with different job titles, people of different ethnic backgrounds, people who worked in the different departments and buildings of the college, faculty members from different departments, administration and staff members of different ranks, and students. All of the panel members were designated to receive complaints.

The third objective was to educate the college community about their rights and responsibilities under the new policy. As an educational institution, Hunter College had the advantage of being fully equipped to launch a community-wide educational and training program. Community education would be a central theme, and so faculty members would lead the panel.

The fourth objective was to foster dialogue and to raise the community's level of awareness about how to prevent sexual harassment. This looked a lot like education, but it was not the same thing. We wanted to address the so-called women's perspective and the so-called men's perspective in a sharing of ideas and with a view toward changing values. Appointing two faculty members as co-coordinators, a male and a female, to partner in the lead role, was the perfect solution. Our educational and awareness program would be sourced by a male–female partnership, and every aspect of the program would reflect the blend, balance, and challenge of that partnership.

The panel was the central group within the college community responsible for raising awareness about sexual harassment and where any employee or student could go to someone with whom they were comfortable speaking. I trained the panel members in sexual harassment law, investigative procedures, and other issues. The panel met regularly, stayed abreast of changing legal requirements, took on their own ongoing training, investigated complaints swiftly, shared with each other and the administration what they learned about concerns of employees and students, and became vigorous advocates for the policy and a harassment-free environment at Hunter College. They developed strong working relationships within the administration, spearheaded the addition of new support services for students, became an important source of recommendations for further actions to improve the program, and enjoyed the respect and confidence of the various campus constituencies.

We were fortunate to have had a forward-thinking president who was willing to try something new. President Donna Shalala lent her full support, critical thinking, political genius, and helpful resources to the new sexual harassment panel. Our committed and energetic original co-coordinators, Professors Michele Paludi and Richard Barickman, breathed life into the plan and later contributed to the academic literature about sexual harassment on campus and its causes. The sexual harassment panel fulfills the same role at Hunter College as it once did and is now called the Sexual Harassment Awareness and Intake Committee.

Today, the City University of New York requires each of its 20 constituent colleges to have a sexual harassment panel as part of its sexual harassment policy and procedures.

A New Language for Relating

What we've got here is a failure to communicate.

—Luke in *Cool Hand Luke*

Lawyers naturally tend to go to the legal system to resolve everything. Lawyers look for a rule, a process, and a remedy. It is the way law school taught us to think. The legal system defines our legal relationships to one another. It can also level the playing field when an ordinary person, such as a target, challenges a more powerful entity, such as an employer, to enforce a legal right. The threat of legal action can be useful in negotiations over legal rights. Many sexual harassment and other complaints are negotiated and settled because one or both parties are unwilling to go to court.

The legal system and legal remedies are not good choices, however, when a situation could be resolved with a simple conversation. I am not suggesting that all situations that involve sexual harassment can be resolved with a conversation. However, the vast majority of situations involving sexual harassment can be resolved satisfactorily with a request to stop.

What if we could dispose of the majority of sexual harassment concerns and complaints simply and easily? What if we, as employees and coworkers, could make them disappear with a few words? What if the employer's sexual harassment complaint and investigation process were allowed to deal with complaints that were serious or could not be resolved with a conversation?

Unfortunately, there are obstacles to this simple proposal. One obstacle is the point of view that all gender-based interaction in the workplace is sexual harassment and should be punished. Another obstacle is the point of view that the only thing that will alter offensive gender-based behavior is an employer's zero-tolerance policy accompanied by uniformly stiff penalties. Other obstacles include the perspectives of many people that a request to change behavior will have a negative affect on working relationships, that people will not honor requests to change behavior, that people should not have to be responsible for communicating what is offensive to them, and a general unwillingness and lack of skills to engage in clear honest workplace communication about personal boundaries.

The Opportunity

Until now, I have talked about reacting to and preventing sexual harassment. The real opportunity is to create something new in the workplace environment, instead of merely eliminating something. My mother, a former math professor, is fond of saying, "You can't really tell someone to not do something. People can relate to 'something,' but they can't relate to 'not something.'" The reason is "something" is always there in "not something." She tells the story of instructing her grandson not to let the dog come in the house. Shortly afterward, she looked up, and there was the dog coming in the door following her grandson. He said, "I tried to not let him in."

When we work hard to respond to, prevent, and avoid sexual harassment, we still have our attention on sexual harassment. If the goal is to rid the workplace of sexual harassment, then we will always be looking for it and we will always find it. Instead of avoiding sexual harassment, we end up with it anyway. What will it take from us to have something else? We would have to be creating something else, something new. I propose creating a workplace culture that is consistent with the reason people are there: to work. I offer a workplace where people experience dignity and respect, a workplace where everyone can thrive. You may want to create something else for your work environment. For example, your objective could be to create a workplace where people operate with passion, commitment, and joy, where people communicate openly and produce results at unprecedented levels, or where people are supported to get their work done.

Whatever environment you are creating, you and the people you work with would have to be operating differently to realize that new environment.

Create an Objective

What kind of environment are you creating? Whatever you and your fellow workers create needs to be an objective that inspires you and that you are willing to have. Creating a new work environment will require people who work together to have conversations about the kind of work environment they want. The conversations could be with the people in your unit, with the people on your hallway, or with your office mate. They could be conversations with the entire organization. You would have a conversation in which you say what kind of environment you want and how you will create that environment for one another. Periodically, you would ask whether you are really creating that environment for one another and whether everyone's experience matches the objective you created. For most of us, creating an objective for the work environment will be a new way of operating.

A New Language for Relating

Everyone who works in your organization, company, shop, or agency had to learn a new language to be effective at his or her job. Whether it is the language of computers, medicine, trucking, packaging, or sales, language is critical to a community and to having results. I don't mean language, such as English or Spanish words, that allow you to communicate anything at all, but language as in specific terms, common meanings, particular ways of expressing yourself, and being assured that the other people understand your meaning when you speak.

In every organization, people need to be competent in the language of their industry, discipline, or job. It is obvious when this kind of job-related language is lacking. The consequences are apparent. Most of us have learned to live without an effective language for relating. We think the consequences of relating ineffectively are inevitable. They are not inevitable.

People can learn to relate effectively and to treat one another with dignity and respect. It is a skill. It takes a few people starting to learn and use the new skills. Eventually a critical mass of people learning and using the new skills will have a powerful impact on the workplace. It could take a very long time. When management intentionally gives people an opportunity to learn the new skills, and when people in the workplace demand that one another learn the new skills, the nature of the workplace can evolve in a dramatically short period of time.

The new language for relating can have effects in your organization that go far beyond how people deal with sexual harassment. It can also have surprising results in productivity, attendance, career advancement, staff relations and, ultimately, profits and personal satisfaction.

The new language for relating requires certain shifts in how we express ourselves with other.

Ask questions

The first shift in language is to ask questions. One of the big problems people have with the definition of sexual harassment is not really a problem with the definition. The problem is how to apply the definition in practical circumstances. It is not possible to know whether your behavior is causing sexual harassment unless you have some idea of how your behavior is affecting or will affect another person. You would have to know the experience of the other person. Specifically, you would have to know whether your actions are interfering with the other person's work performance or causing the other person to experience the work environment as hostile, offensive, or intimidating. Even if you know how your actions are affecting the other person, you cannot assume that they will affect someone else the same way. You know they might affect the other person the same way, but you cannot be certain. This leaves people uncertain, and we don't like uncertainty.

Asking questions allows you to know the other person's experience. Start asking questions such as, "What's it like for you when the guys joke about your bra size? Do you think that's funny? Are you offended?"

Speak up

The second shift in language is to speak up. Speak up for yourself. Speak up when you do not understand what is going on, when something is not working, and when you do not know what to do. I do not mean telling people off or just stating your opinion to state it. I mean speaking up to shift the course of events.

The *Wall Street Journal* reported a survey that revealed black people do not share their experience with white people and then are surprised when white people don't understand or appreciate their experience. There is a similar phenomenon with men and women, where women do not share their experience with men and then are surprised that men neither understand, nor appreciate, their experience and the effect of certain behavior on women's experience.

Speaking up is sharing your experience with another, not to blame, to criticize, to characterize, or "to blow off steam," but to give you and the other person an opportunity to deal honestly with each other. When you communicate your concerns and personal boundaries, you allow others to relate with you responsibly.

Pay attention

The third shift in language is to pay attention, and more specifically, to give others the sense that you are paying attention to them. How would you do that? One way is to say, "This is what I heard you say. Is that what you said?" A supervisor who follows the advice in Chapter 7 is making sure the employee has the sense the supervisor is paying attention.

Have you ever noticed when someone says the same thing to you repeatedly? Usually, when people repeat what they said, it is because they think you didn't hear them.

This third shift will require some of us to admit that we are not terribly interested in what other people have to say. We are interested in what we are going to say next or how to get our point across. We say we are paying attention when we are not.

Make requests

The fourth shift in the new language calls for making requests and getting responses to your requests. You would say specifically what the other person did, that it was unwelcome, and that you are requesting that he or she stop and never do it again. You then pay attention and wait for a response. If he or she agrees, thank the person. If he or she doesn't, ask for a response. If the person says anything other than yes, submit a complaint. If he or she does it again, submit a complaint.

This is a subtle shift for some of us. You would be surprised how often we do not make a request when we are really doing something else.

We give the reasons we want something, but we do not ask for it.

We say, "It's awfully warm in here," versus "Please turn the heat down."

We threaten: "If you don't stop harassing me, I'm going to report you," rather than saying, "It makes me uncomfortable when you touch me during our meetings. Please don't do that anymore."

We complain, "I can't stand it when you interrupt meeting. I can't get a complete sentence out," versus "John, you interrupted me again. Would you let me finish what I was saying before you start speaking?"

We accuse: "I can't believe you just said that! Where do you get off treating me like that? What's the matter with you?"

Requests get action. They state a specific action to be done or a specific action to stop.

Get a response to your request

The fifth shift is to get a response to your request. A request calls for a response. You would have to pay attention to what the other person says in response to your request. You would be surprised how often people don't get responses to their requests. In the course of investigations and consultations, I have asked dozens of people, "What did she say in response when you asked her to stop?" The most common answers are, "She didn't say anything," and "I don't know what she said."

You would have to ask the following questions:

- "Do you accept my request?"
- "Do you agree to do what I asked?"

Speak with a purpose

The sixth shift in language is to speak with a purpose. Speaking with a purpose involves more than thinking before you speak. Purpose is an aim that guides action. Speaking with a purpose is speaking consciously with an intention or with an objective. You would have to know why you are speaking before you speak. Most of us have a thought or a feeling and then we let whatever thought is there pop out of our mouths. We confuse our thoughts and feelings for a purpose or objective.

Use nonjudgmental language

Judgmental language puts people on the defensive and eliminates any possibility of having an effective conversation that could shift the course of events. Judgmental language states a conclusion or your opinion about a person or the person's behavior, instead of just saying what happened and requesting that the person stop. Judgmental language includes the following terms: sexual harassment, sexual harasser, victim, guilty, predator, conspiracy, sexist, unfair, discriminatory, and violation.

Actors use similar judgmental language, but usually with the word "not": not sexual harassment, not a sexual harasser, not a victim, not guilty, not a predator, not a conspiracy, not sexist, not unfair, not discriminatory, and not a violation. Actors have additional terms: touchy, oversensitive, sheltered, no sense of humor/humorless, straight-laced, puritanical, vindictive, unrealistic, picky, and imaginative.

For example, calling someone's behavior "sexual harassment" creates a debate over whether he or she is, in fact, engaging in sexual harassment and puts the conversation in an adversarial mode. It is now "you versus the other person" or "your view versus his or her view." In the moment, all that matters is that the behavior is unwelcome and you want it to stop.

Create time for learning

As you move into a new way of relating, create time for learning and expect to make mistakes. You may notice that you did not make a request when a request was called for. You may have to go back and say, "I realized I didn't make a request." You may forget to wait for a response. You may have to go back and say, "I didn't hear your response to my request, and I don't know whether you are going to do what I asked. Will you do what I asked?"

It may feel awkward at first. It will take time to get used to clear purposeful speaking. You may feel awkward at first, especially if you have spent your entire life thinking people should know what you want without your having to ask for it.

What does any of this have to do with sexual harassment?

Most situations that involve sexual harassment or potentially involve sexual harassment could be addressed simply and directly in the moment. Other situations require more drastic action, such as a formal complaint and corrective actions on the part of the employer. If we can separate the two, we could address the people who engage in severe harassment and abuse supervisory authority. We could make a concerted and creative effort to affect the behavior of a few people.

The purpose here is to allow you to take charge of the action, before the lawyers take charge. You can shift the course of events in the moment the action is happening by paying attention, communicating effectively, making requests, and getting responses.

Value everyone's workplace experience

Value everyone in the workplace and how they feel about working there. Value your own environment as a place where you want to come. If your work environment is offensive, intimidating, or hostile, there are actions take.

The Role of the Active Observer

Active observers may have the greatest opportunity to affect sexual harassment in the workplace. Contrary to the commonly held belief that virtually all sexual harassment occurs in private, active observers see and hear a great deal that others think goes unobserved. They observe how people are feeling. They hear what people are bragging about. They recall who hasn't shown up for work a few days in a row. They know who is thinking about asking for a transfer. They also see the state in which a fellow worker returns from a meeting, lunch, or business trip.

Active observers do not have to watch powerlessly as work relationships between their colleagues deteriorate. An active observer can make responsible inquiries. They can ask a target how he or she felt about a particular remark or ask the actor what the intention was in doing what he or she did. An active observer can stop the action by saying, "Something is unclear here" or "What you just said is off base."

An active observer can encourage inappropriate behavior by saying and doing nothing when they see behavior that violates the policy. People interpret silence as agreement or consent. If, as an active observer, you remain silent when you observe offensive behavior directed toward a fellow employee, the actor will assume you do not object to, or worse, that you approve of the behavior.

> If you are an active observer
>
> ☑ Listen to your fellow employees.
> ☑ Educate yourself.
> ☑ Dare to speak up.
> ☑ Affirm your own standards.
> ☑ Encourage Targets to speak up.
> ☑ Report sexual harassment you observe.

Regardless of the role you are in, remaining silent when you have something to say has consequences. Sexual harassment continues in the workplace only because someone is tolerating it.

Appendix

Self-Test

Indicate True or False

_____ 1. A romantic consensual relationship is permitted, so long as the supervisor and the subordinate report their relationship to management.

_____ 2. Men cannot be sexually harassed because men always enjoy sexual attention from women.

_____ 3. An employee can be harassed by another employee of the same sex only if the other employee is a homosexual.

_____ 4. Questions, jokes, and comments can be sexually harassing, even if there has been no touching.

_____ 5. An employee can complain about unwelcome sexual behavior that interferes with his or her work performance or is intimidating, hostile, or offensive.

_____ 6. An employee who believes he or she has been sexually harassed must report behavior to his or her immediate supervisor.

_____ 7. Before an employee can complain about being sexually harassed, he or she must be able to prove that the behavior was sexual harassment.

_____ 8. If an employee complains and it is later determined that he or she wasn't sexually harassed, the complaining employee will be disciplined.

_____ 9. Only a supervisor can sexually harass an employee.

_____ 10. The sexual harassment policy does not apply to employees who have never harassed anyone in the past.

_____ 11. It is never sexual harassment for a naturally affectionate or expressive person to pat or touch another employee, even if the other person doesn't want to be touched, so long as it isn't meant to be sexual or offensive.

_____ 12. An employee should never initiate a conversation with someone who has harassed him or her.

• • •

Self-Test Answers

1.	False	5.	True	9.	False
2	False	6.	False	10.	False
3.	False	7	False	11.	False
4.	True	8.	False	12.	False

Index

About the Author

LINDA GORDON HOWARD has spent the last 30 years successfully practicing, advising, counseling, and teaching in the area of employment discrimination and sexual harassment law. She has trained thousands of employees in how to understand and comply with the difficult and confusing law of sexual harassment. Her original and proven methods communicate the logic behind the law and illustrate how to deal with sexual harassment as it happens.

Ms. Howard received her law degree from the University of Virginia Law School and undergraduate degree from Reed College. She is a former law professor, member of the White House Staff, college legal counsel, and senior attorney for the City of New York. She serves as a Trustee of Reed College and a Director of the not-for-profit A More Perfect Union, Inc. and leads transformational programs for Landmark Education. She practices law in New York City.